Secret Stories of Extinct Walt Disney World

The World That Disappeared

Jim Korkis

Theme Park Press
The Happiest Books on Earth
www.ThemeParkPress.com

Theme Park Press publishes its books in a variety of print and electronic formats. Some content that appears in one format may not appear in another.

Editor: Bob McLain
Layout: Artisanal Text

ISBN 979-8-89609-050-2
Printed in the United States of America

Theme Park Press | www.ThemeParkPress.com
Address queries to ben@themeparkpress.com

Dedicated to my brothers Michael and Chris who like myself worked at Walt Disney World during the past thirty years and watched so much of it go extinct while we weren't paying attention.

CONTENTS

Introduction

For those who love Walt Disney World, it means having to learn to live with constant lost as things continually change or are removed often without warning. Few things last beyond twenty years at WDW without removal or significant redesigning.

In its first half century, WDW has seen countless beloved things vanish into the mists of memory. Recent years have seen a rapid and massive demolition of much of Disney's Hollywood Studios and Epcot to make room for new additions from a mythological galaxy far, far away to an ambitious rat who became a renowned chef.

These new additions always come at a cost beyond the monetary investment by the loss of familiar old favorites.

In 2019, I wrote a book about the extinct things of Disneyland that became popular not only for those who had experienced them but to tantalize the curiosity of others who might have only briefly heard about them if they knew they had ever existed at all.

As WDW's anniversary approaches, I realized that it was time to do a similar book detailing some of the things that no longer can be found at Walt Disney World but at one time provided magical memories. I was fortunate to experience most of the things in this book so that helped with providing an accurate perspective.

Just like the vanished things at Walt Disney World, the websites that document them often disappear as well. I find that a book, despite its limitations to make instanteous additions and corrections, is a wonderful vehicle to preserve this information.

So many things have disappeared over the decades that there was no way to include all of them but I have attempted to include as many favorites as well as some oddball things as space would allow. In some chapters, I tried to shoehorn in additional information about related things.

The challenge was what to include and what to leave out. If CommuniCore gets its own chapter, then should Innoventions?

If I use the space to write about the Diamond Horseshoe Revue is it then okay to leave out the Mike Fink Keel Boats because there is no more space to include it?

What if an attraction remained much the same but did receive a different make-over and a new name like Flight to the Moon becoming Mission to Mars? Hard choices had to be made but hopefully if this book sells well then there will be a sequel so I can include what was left on the cutting room floor.

The chapters here are just a brief snapshot and much more could and should be written about each example. One of the other challenges was in assigning dates to these things because Disney was not always diligent in recording such dates or would do "soft openings and closings" or even after closing something might unexpectedly re-open it for a brief period of time to accommodate an increase in attendance.

Walt Disney World is not a museum but a living entity (and a thriving business) that changes and grows to adapt to the needs and wants of its current audience. Things that were once considered innovative and revolutionary are now seen as out-of-date compared to new advances in technology. Things that were once popular are no longer familiar which is why Winnie the Pooh could so easily oust Mr. Toad from his location.

However, many of us like myself are nostalgic for the simpler treats that made our visits to the Orlando vacation destination so memorable and magical. This book documents some of them before they are completely forgotten and reveal behind-the-scenes information about them that may not be widely known.

When I first started writing this book, it never occurred to me that the entire Walt Disney World might go extinct for seemingly endless weeks because of the outbreak of the coronavirus and that many things I took for granted might change drastically or even disappear when it did finally return. That's another good reason to try to fully appreciate everything when we visit Walt Disney World because everything is only temporary.

Enjoy this brief time travel trip. Please remain seated and keep your arms and legs inside the book at all time and no smoking or flash photography please....even if that was an accepted practice in some of the good ol' days recounted here.

Jim Korkis / Disney Historian
May 2020

Magic Kingdom

The Magic Kingdom opened October 1, 1971 and its iconic Cinderella Castle is recognized around the world. Inspired by California's Disneyland, it is the most popular of the four WDW parks and welcomes over twenty million guests a year.

When guests think of the many changes that have taken place during the last half century, they usually focus on vanished attractions or food and beverage locations. Sadly, many, many smaller details disappeared quietly as well including the following items that delighted guests:

On Main Street U.S.A., the Crystal Arts shop used to have what looked like a beveled glass sign with its name hanging over the doorway. The name could be read clearly and yet when guests walked underneath it to the other side they found they could still read the name clearly and the lettering was not backwards. The sign was actually a mirror reflecting the overhang so that it seemed like guests could look through it like a piece of glass.

The Car Barn in Town Square used to be open to guests so they could come in and visit with one of the horses in the stall. They could also see an authenic Edison light bulb, handmade by a man in Virginia that cost WDW eight dollars each. The authentic light switch for it had one protruding prong with mother-of-pearl coating so someone could tell "on" and "off" even in the dark.

A real cavalry lantern was placed on an upper shelf to indicate this was a place of horses. On the walls were vintage stone tablets that could be heated up in the pot bellied stove and wrapped in blankets for hay rides on a cold night. Authentic harnesses were displayed as well as other details like reproductions of antique veterinarian notices.

The original Tomorrowland had an entirely different entrance with two distinctive nearly one hundred foot tall white towers where jets of water flowed down into the hub canal on either side of the land's bridgeway and created a pleasant mist.

The land was rehabbed in 1994 and in 1999 a Metrophone booth from the Galactic Communications Network (GCN) was installed. By randomly punching several numbers brought up a loop with one of nine possible hilarious one-sided conversations from Rocket Realty, Sonny Eclipse's agent Johnny Jupiter, Earth Crust Pizza, Intergalactic Movie Line, Psychic Robots Network, and more including the time and weather from Corona Borealis of the Tomorrowland News Network. It was quietly removed in recent years.

Also removed near the entrance to the TTA PeopleMover was the Robo-Newz vendor whose main case showed the latest issue of the *Galaxy Gazette* with the headline: "Stitch Escapes!"

Liberty Square's entrance changed as well. In 1971, the Court of Flags representing the original 13 states led guests to the old Concord Bridge, where the colonial forces faced off with the British in 1775. In 1991, those flags were relocated to surround the Liberty Bell that had been installed in 1989. The entrance to the land was rebuilt with the brick walls, plaque and guardhouse that are familiar today. Stanchions now fill the holes where the flagpoles once stood.

The Tinker Bell's Treasures shop in Fantasyland was divided into two sections. One was designed like the bedroom of the Darling children. Guests could awaken the fairy Tinker Bell who thanks to fiber optic technology would fly around the room into the second section designed like the upper deck of Captain Hook's pirate ship with a wooden floor. In 2010, the store was remodeled to become part of Castle Couture with a Bibbidi Bobbidi Boutique.

Gulf Hospitality House

(1971 – 1990)

In place of Disneyland's famed Opera House, the Magic Kingdom had what is now called the Town Square Theater.

When the Magic Kingdom opened in 1971, that beautiful building was officially the elegant Main Street Hotel that housed the Gulf Hospitality Center sponsored by Gulf. The legendary Dorothea Redmond had created concept art for the possibility of building an actual upscale Victorian hotel on Main Street that would have extended through the building's two theaters as well as to what became a cast parking lot behind the Tomorrowland stage.

Some of those design elements of a hotel still remain including the individual balconies on the upper floor windows and the broad front porch with rocking chairs. Since the Walt Disney Company had never operated a hotel before and the development of plans for an elaborate series of nearby themed hotels beginning with the Contemporary and the Polynesian Village managed by an outside business, it resulted in the idea of an in-park hotel being cancelled.

According to the original storyline, it was located next to the Train Station so that people would have a place to stay while they waited for their train connection or visiting the city.

When the Magic Kingdom opened in 1971, this beautiful building was the unofficial central location for all of Walt Disney property, where guests could make reservations for resort rooms, dinner shows, golfing and other recreational activities.

The large, polished wooden counter was primarily staffed by friendly and attractive young women who extolled the virtues of Gulf Oil, of course, and handed out maps and brochures that assisted guests with driving routes, places to visit in Central Florida and selecting hotels or motels at which to stay on their trip.

In addition to the service stations located on the property for both guests and employees, Gulf Oil had exclusive rights for oil products used on the property as it did at Disneyland.

"Etched glass doors, potted palms, comfortable velvet settees and antique chairs set the mood for relaxation and comfort," claimed the 1972 "Gulf Personal Tourguide (sic) to Walt Disney World," describing the Hospitality Center.

It was a full-sized building rather than utilizing forced perspective because it was necessary to block the guests' view of the Contemporary resort, which would have conflicted with the theme of Main Street. The Contemporary was still clearly visible in Tomorrowland because it had a vaguely futuristic look that didn't detract from the "world of the immediate future" theme.

Opening in April 1973 as part of the building was the *Walt Disney Story*, a 28-minute film presentation featuring excerpts with narration from old interviews with Walt Disney to provide his autobiography.

The Hospitality House officially closed March 1990 and became Disneyana Collectibles store. It later became the Town Square Exposition Hall in 1998 and closed in 2011 to reopen as the Town Square Theater.

The Town Square Exposition Hall was both a mini museum of cameras and photography, presenting the history of cameras and how they have been used in the movie-industry and a small theatre (cinema) showing the *Milestones in Animation* film with classic Disney animated shorts.

The area was sponsored by Kodak and the gift shop allowed guests the opportunity to purchase many film and camera related products and services including using a digital media card to burn the images onto a CD. In addition there were large photo displays of Disney animated scenes where guests could insert themselves and take a picture.

The Walt Disney Story
(1973 – 1992)

The Walt Disney Story opened in April 1973 in a section on the southwest side of the Gulf Hospitality House on Main Street. It was sponsored by Gulf until 1979.

The pre-show lobby area was filled with fascinating artifacts honoring Walt's long career. Included were letters from celebrities and political figures, photographs depicting achievements in live-action and animation as well as television. The eight-Oscar presented to Walt for *Snow White and the Seven Dwarfs* (1937) was on display along with a scale model of the Nautilus submarine from *20,000 Leagues Under the Sea* (1954).

At the end of the hallway were the entrances to two identical 300 seat theaters. Between the entrances on a curved section of wall that jutted outward was a mural created especially for this WDW attraction by animator and Imagineer Bill Justice. It featured 170 Disney characters and used 1,200 separate colors.

Up until the mid-1980s, characters from more recent releases including *The Black Cauldron*, *The Great Mouse Detective*, *The Fox and the Hound*, *Pete's Dragon*, and *The Rescuers* were added to the mural by artist Russell Schroeder.

Schroeder also painted an oval gold emblem with the following quote by Walt Disney. It was set in a space that was originally left purposely empty for a cast member to stand on a slightly raised platform, so it looked like they were surrounded by characters as they welcomed guests to the film.

> To translate the world's great fairy tales, thrilling legends, stirring folk tales into visual theatrical presentations and to get back the warm response of audiences in many lands has been for me an experience and a lifetime satisfaction beyond value. —Walt Disney

In the main theater, a twenty-eight minute biographical film of Walt Disney's personal and professional life from his birth to the creation of the Florida Project that included rare stills and film clips was a project that began in June 1969.

When The Walt Disney Story closed in 1992, guest access to view the mural became more limited. In 1998, the building became the Main Street Exposition Hall and the mural was placed off limits with the entrance to it concealed behind a curtain.

In 2012, the interior was re-designed as the Main Street Town Square Theater for a Mickey Mouse meet-and-greet location. During the conversion, an attempt was made to save the mural, but not all of it was able to be preserved when it was removed from the wall.

A staff of more than 200 people at Walt Disney Productions pored over 75 hours of interviews conducted with Walt before his untimely death on December 15, 1966 to produce the film.

Bill Bosche, an artist and producer who worked for Disney for more than thirty years supervised the work. By using excerpts from these interviews, in particular the extensive 1956 ones done with *Saturday Evening Post* writer Pete Martin, Walt Disney posthumously narrated much of his own autobiography.

The film was presented as a virtual photo scrapbook of Walt's life. It was projected through an anamorphic lens which enabled a screen proportion of 2.67 to 1. A severly edited version was later released briefly on VHS and DVD in a pan-and-scan format.

In October 1992, the attraction was closed with Disney citing deterioration of the original film print but others suggesting that low attendance and saving on operating costs were the main reasons.

Bill Justice Mural

(1973 – 2012)

Bill Justice began his career at Disney as an animator on Donald Duck and Chip'n'Dale theatrical animated shorts. He was moved over to Imagineering as a designer of attractions, parades and programmer of audio-animatronics figures.

Justice was tasked with creating a huge mural featuring the most memorable Disney animated characters to entertain guests waiting to enter the theaters for The Walt Disney Story.

Back in 1991, I talked with Justice about this unique mural's creation:

> I did a mural with 170 Disney characters and the final painted version was twenty-four feet long and eight and a half feet high. The company was worried about it getting dirty and fingerprints and mustard and ketchup and all that kind of stuff all over it. It turned out that people for some reason kind of respect it and it looks like it was freshly painted. It was done on canvas and then glued to the wall.

> I did a rendering that's five feet long and twenty-four inches high that was copied by Clem Hall and a couple of his assistants at the Disney Studio in what they call a "scene easel." That's a great big frame and there's a pit and you can raise and lower the final eight and a half foot canvas down into that pit and you can paint along the top of it. You can move it up a little bit until you get it up here and finally you are painting the bottom of it. Instead of being on a ladder and painting, this makes it real easy.

> They just stand on the floor and the image is always at eye level. They've got their paints over here and their brushes and everything and they project the thing on to this big canvas, make a line drawing and then they followed my color scheme for each figure and so forth. Basically, they traced my figures using the projector onto the canvas. The mural took almost four months to complete.

> All I had to do before the painting was shipped from the Studio to Florida was some minor touch-up work.
>
> Once it was all installed, I got a phone call. Somebody had complained that their favorite character was not on the mural. It was the Cheshire Cat. I guess I was feeling feisty or creative but I immediately responded that the cat was there. He is invisible like he is in the film and is in the upper right hand corner of the painting. He could only be seen on Tuesday and Thursday nights at 2 a.m. when the park was closed. After that, I didn't receive any more complaints.

During the conversion of the area in 2012, an attempt was made to save the mural but was not entirely successful especially with some of artist Russell Schroeder's later additions of newer characters done outside the original canvas being lost in the process. It is now stored in the Disney Archives.

In 1993, a limited edition (only 1200 copies) lithograph print of the mural was produced for sale exclusively to Disney cast members. This was considered a Printer's Proof and marked accordingly with Justice signing each print at the lower right.

To honor that well-remembered piece of artwork, in the new Town Square Theater as the guests move along the queue to meet Mickey, a rolled up print of the Bill Justice mural can be seen in a mail slot labelled "B. Justice".

Baby Care Center Art

(1976 – CIRCA 2000)

There once was mural artwork done by Disney Legend Bill Justice that decorated the inside of the Baby Care Center near Casey's Corner off of Main Street U.S.A. in the Magic Kingdom. This Center is the largest one in the four theme parks, and offers the opportunity for changing diapers, feeding, potty training, purchasing items and more.

Today, the interior of that location has striped wallpaper to theme in with the design of Main Street U.S.A. with some Plexiglas full-colored images of classic Disney characters overlaid in a handful of spots.

For over two decades there was different artwork that greeted parents and their children as they sought the services for the unique location. From an interview I did with Justice in 1991, here are his memories of that unusual assignment:

> In January 1976, Walt Disney World built a Baby Station just around the corner from Main Street, but they were upset that it looked too much like a doctor's office. So I asked for a copy of the plans for the four rooms. When I submitted my proposal for adding artwork, it was immediately approved and I found myself on a plane to Florida in March 1976.
>
> I actually painted right on the wall. The wallpaper is a kind of a plastic with a little tooth in it and can be washed and stuff so that it was easy to keep clean. That's the reason they chose it rather than regular wallpaper. I did it in a technique called dry brush but it's wet paint on a brush, but it shows a little bit of texture through the line. I just did it in a brown line on the wall.
>
> It's a real nice baby station, much better than the one at Disneyland because it has four rooms and a kitchen and a couple of ladies that work there that are in uniform, so they kind of look like maids. They can warm the baby's bottles in the kitchen and

stuff and then they have a room where they change the diapers and they have little almost like small bunks.

It's a real nice facility. And each wall in each room has a Pinocchio and Jiminy Cricket and maybe a Geppetto on maybe one wall and a scene from *Dumbo* on another wall and maybe a scene from *Fantasia* on this wall. Each wall has a center picture that represents one of our films.

As you enter, like a picture in a children's book that shows "Welcome to Baby Land", Goofy's painting it and Donald Duck's watching him and a couple of little Dalmatian puppies are looking into the paint and one puppy's running away leaving brown footprints. There are puppies all around every wall.

Every wall has several puppies and footprints that go a certain height above the floor and puppies are running up the wall and sitting on top of the door and looking down like can't get down and things like this.

As you exit, on a wall that you pass, a small little jog in the wall, Mickey says 'Have a Nice Day' and a couple of Dalmatian puppies down below. Somebody counted and there are 74 Dalmatian puppies in these four rooms all together and there's something like 1,268 footprints and 34 other Disney characters. People that write, authors when they write an article or something, they've got to know statistics. I painted it all right on site.

Unfortunately, these murals were covered over when the location was refurbished into a more contemporary venue.

Mickey Mouse Revue
(1971 – 1980)

The very first theme park attraction with Mickey Mouse was the signature attraction at the Magic Kingdom in Florida when it opened in 1971 called The Mickey Mouse Revue created primarily by Disney Legend Bill Justice, who told me in an interview:

> [Walt Disney Imagineering] had designed some imaginative shows for the parks, but we seemed to be getting away from our heritage. What we needed was a reminder of what Walt had accomplished. I pulled out a sheet of paper and got to work. Mickey Mouse would have to be the main figure.
>
> The show we had in mind was this: Mickey Mouse would lead an orchestra of Studio characters through a medley of Disney tunes. He had led orchestras in many of his cartoons so it seemed a natural fit. Then on the sides of the stage and behind the orchestra, scenes from our most popular animated features would appear one by one. Mickey and his orchestra would close the performance.
>
> One big problem surfaced: Mickey. With 33 functions crammed into a 42-inch body, he was the most complex audio-animatronics figure to date. He also became my biggest programming challenge because I had to do extreme movements so it would appear that Mickey was keeping up with the tempo.

Imagineers John Hench and Blaine Gibson were also significantly involved in the show. There was an eight minute pre-show featuring an overview of Mickey's animated career as well as the use of sound in animation.

There were a total of seventy-three different Disney animated characters who performed in the show from the Fab Five to Humphrey the Bear, Timothy Mouse, Winnie the Pooh, Baloo, Scrooge McDuck and many, many more that filled the 86-foot-long stage. However, there were a total of 81 figures since some characters appeared at different places on the stage, like the Three Caballeros, or in different costumes.

Justice said:

> Roy O. Disney looked the finished model over, then paid me the best compliment I ever had in my career: 'This is the kind of show we should spend our money on.'

The attraction closed at Walt Disney World on September 14, 1980 and was moved to Tokyo Disneyland where it was an opening day attraction April 1983 and continued to operate until May 2009.

Justice recalled:

> The theater seated 504 people, but the space available for the pre-show could only accommodate 300 because of a mistake that someone had made. Unfortunately, there was no time or money left to make further changes. It came as a shock when I was told my pride and joy was being moved to Tokyo Disneyland. 'Because it never played to full capacity'. Of course not! How can you fill 504 seats with 300 people?

> Tokyo Disneyland wanted it because it was so cute. It saved the Disney Company money because it was a complete attraction that was shipped directly to Japan rather than being replicated. It helped make the opening deadline on time. It would have been time consuming and expensive to build it from scratch in Tokyo. It was the first attraction closed at the Magic Kingdom.

At the Magic Kingdom, the building eventually became the home to another Mickey attraction, Mickey's PhilharMagic that opened in 2003 where once again Mickey is leading an orchestra although he only appears briefly in the show.

20,000 Leagues Under the Sea

(1971 – 1994)

20,000 Leagues Under the Sea was a popular Disney 1954 live action feature film adventure that told the tale of the mysterious Captain Nemo and his Nautilus submarine and the many perils encountered in the ocean's depths.

Submarine Voyage was one of the first "E Ticket" attractions at Disneyland in 1959 where eight submarines designed and named for the existing U.S. nuclear submarine fleet took guests on an underwater journey.

Imagineer Tony Baxter as Imagineer Claude Coats' apprentice was in charge of significantly reimagining it into Nemo's story with twelve submarines, each accomodating forty people, that resembled the classic Harper Goff Victorian designed Nautilus from the Disney live action film.

Cast members operating the attraction wore replicas of the uniforms from the film. Voice artist Pete Renoudet mimicked James Mason's tone from the film for the narration by Captain Nemo.

Doing all this made this attraction more of a fantasy rather than appropriate for Tomorrowland so it was situated in Fantasyland (taking up 20% of the area) in an 11.5 million gallon lagoon.

The sixty-one foot long subs originally ran on natural gas, but were converted to Perkins diesel engines within the first ten years providing a distinct smell at the attraction.

The voyage was similar to the one at Disneyland where the ship would "probe depths seldom seen by man" and "pass below the polar ice cap". Guests peered out of a porthole in front of them and were able to see assorted sea animals like fish with limited animation elements. The underwater denizens could be heard thanks to Nemo's sonar hydrophone technology.

Underwater divers harvested "the abundance that nature has sown beneath the sea." In the Disneyland version, the divers were salvaging treasure from shipwrecks. Surface storms drove the vessel lower just in time to catch a glimpse of an octopus wrestling a shark. After a bout of blackness, guests could see the ocean floor littered with a graveyard of shipwrecks that could not avoid storms.

The Nautilus then navigated under the polar ice cap viewing fish in "a realm of eternal darkness" thanks to black light effects. Rising to a more sensible depth, guests saw the remains of an ancient civilization that was implied to be Atlantis destroyed by an erupting volcano. Nemo claimed the existence of such a continent was fantasy "along with the legends of sea serpents and mermaids" which, of course, prompted the appearance of a green sea serpent with googly eyes along with a trio of mermaids and treasures.

The rumblings of an underwater volcano getting ready to erupt sends the ship in a hurried rush back to the surface and in the process a glimpse of one of Nemo's fleet being crushed like an eggshell by a giant red squid. Another squid attacked the Nautilus but an electrical charge drove it away and the ship returned to the placid lagoon.

The attraction closed in September 1994 supposedly for a refurbishment but never reopened. High maintenance costs and operational budget, slow loading, lack of disabled access and limited capacity were often cited as reasons. In 1996, Disney officially announced the attraction was closed.

The submarines were moved backstage where their portholes were popped out and sold at the Disney Store for $125 a piece. The subs were sold to a scrapyard and the fiberglass hulls were buried in landfill. Two of the subs were sent to Castaway Cay and sunk in the snorkeling lagoon while one other was gutted and used for convention events.

Mr. Toad's Wild Ride

(1971 – 1998)

Mr. Toad's Wild Ride was a classic "C Ticket" dark ride in Fantasyland that originated at Disneyland on opening day. Its doppelganger was also an opening day attraction at Magic Kingdom's Fantasyland but closed in 1998 and was replaced by The Many Adventures of Winnie the Pooh.

The ride's story inspired by the Disney animated feature *The Adventures of Ichabod and Mr. Toad* (1949) and focused primarily on Toad's terrifying and irresponsible driving through London going "nowhere in particular".

Guests boarded turn-of-the-last century motorcars individually named for characters in the story. Each vehicle had a quarter horsepower electrical motor drawing power from the rail beneath it.

The Disneyland version was so highly popular that the Imagineers wanted to increase the capacity for the attraction so the Florida ride had two separate tracks and boarding areas. Each track featured some different scenes.

Track One took guests through a library, a rural English barnyard with animals, and through a courtroom and jail cells with convicts. Track Two allowed guests to view Toad's trophy room, a kitchen, a gypsy camp, Ratty's house and Winky's Tavern.

Both tracks took a spin through the town's plaza, circling a fountain and eventually ended on railroad tracks where an approaching train sends the vehicle to "Hell". The guests are greeted by gleeful, little red demons having pitchforks and tails which was a scene not in the film itself but was included because of Walt Disney's personal feeling that reckless driving should have consequences. Officially, the scene was labeled the "Inferno Room" referencing *Dante's Inferno*.

Maintenance costs were minimal. The attraction could accommodate all ages, sizes and any health conditions. In addition, the attraction was what was known as a "push-button" ride that could be operated by any Fantasyland attraction cast member with minimal training. However, it was a slow loading attraction and the effects quickly became out-dated.

Winnie the Pooh and his friends were enjoying a huge surge of popularity while guests did not remember the film inspiration for the Mr. Toad attraction at all and there was no Toad merchandise being sold in the park. On the other hand, Pooh related merchandise was selling more than Mickey Mouse and with the addition of an attraction those sales would only increase. With the Toad's attraction double space there was plenty of room for an attraction and a gift shop. In 1997, Disney announced that a Pooh attraction would replace Toad.

A fan campaign was launched to "Save Toad" headed by John Lefante who urged sending letters and e-mails to the Walt Disney Company by the thousands. That campaign led to actual demonstrations at the attraction called "Toad-Ins" reminiscent of the well-known "sit-ins" and they garnered media attention. Those reports led to even more supporters but the attraction still closed as announced.

In the new attraction on the left wall of the scene in Owl's house, there is a painting of Mr. Toad handing over the deed to the building to Owl and there is also a picture of Mole tipping his hat to Pooh. In the Haunted Mansion pet cemetery, up near the top is the Kevin Kidney Big Fig of Mr. Toad painted to resemble an oxidized, rusting grave marker.

Disneyland Paris was originally meant to have a ride version that would have been truer to the actual film with a different final scene that would have had Toad in a plane. It was never built but a Toad Hall restaurant (with an exterior similar to Disneyland's 1983 attraction) did open.

The Legend of the Lion King
(1994 – 2002)

Disney's animated feature *The Lion King* (1994) was so hugely popular that there were seven different adaptations of the story for different Disney theme parks.

The Lion King Celebration was a parade at Disneyland from 1994-1997. *Festival of the Lion King* show opened in 1998 in Disney's Animal Kingdom. A variation of that show opened in Hong Kong Disneyland in 2005. Disneyland Paris had *The Legend of the Lion King.* That park also debuted *The Lion King: Rhythms of the Pride Lands* in 2019 in Frontierland.

In 2019, Disney California Adventure opened *The Tale of the Lion King* where a narrator leads a troupe of performers called the "Storytellers of the Pride Lands."

For the Magic Kingdom, *The Legend of the Lion King* sponsored by Kodak premiered July 8, 1994 and lasted until February 23, 2002 when it was ousted from its theater in Fantasyland and replaced by *Mickey's PhilharMagic* that opened in October 2003.

This Walt Disney World show was unique in its approach to the story of *The Lion King* since it used huge, over-sized puppets that Disney dubbed "humanimals", a combination of human puppeteers trained by people who had worked with Jim Henson and who operated the animal puppets from a cramped pit space under the stage.

Ten puppeteers did the show three times per hour and it included a pre-show (where the audience had to stand) with a live costumed Rafiki warming up the audience. Rafiki also appeared in the show itself with narration to help the transition between scenes.

The Mufasa figure measured seven feet long from the end of the tail to the top of the head, stood six feet tall and was perched upon an eighteen foot tall Pride Rock. During the course of the show, Simba grows from a two and a half foot cub to a seven foot full grown lion. In one scene it took five puppeteers to do the movements for just one large figure.

The stage itself was 125 feet wide, making it larger than the seating area that could hold five hundred guests. That width was needed for the set pieces that would move in to the viewing area from every direction and depicted the rocky Pride lands of Africa, deep jungle, moonlit watering hole and the Serengeti grasslands. At the back of the stage was a huge oval screen where clips from the animated film were shown at appropriate times during the show.

Show director Fran Soeder who had also directed DHS's *Voyage of the Little Mermaid* and *The Hunchback of Notre Dame* that also utilized puppets, said:

> It's hard to believe they are not live performers in costume. It's like watching an animation 'cel' from the film come to life. Humanimals provide an exciting new way to translate an animated feature into a Disney stage show.
>
> Every element of this show seems to live and breathe, including Africa, where the story takes place. Each and every part of this show interacts with the others, making the audience feel they are in the heart of the film.

The show included the beloved songs from the film on a pre-recorded track including "Circle of Life," "I Can't Wait to Be King," "Be Prepared," "Can You Feel the Love Tonight," and "Hakuna Matata." The cast included Mufassa, Simba, Nala, Scar, Zazu, Pumba, Timon and the hyenas Shenzi, Banzai and Ed.

Sword in the Stone Ceremony

(1993 – 2006)

The great and clever wizard Merlin the magician is a main character in the 1963 Disney animated feature *The Sword in the Stone*.

The walk-around costumed "face character" of Merlin officiated the well-loved Sword in the Stone ceremony several times a day in front of the carousel at Disneyland and the Magic Kingdom, where a guest was selected to draw the fabled sword from the stone — just like the young Arthur who did so and became the King of England.

The show began at Disneyland in summer 1983, the same year Merlin's Magic Shop closed at the park and the new architectural redesign of Fantasyland opened. Disneyland Paris had the ceremony in the castle courtyard beginning in 1992 but it was canceled in 2001, and then later brought back for special holidays and the summer. Hong Kong Disneyland also had a Sword in the Stone ceremony when it opened in 2005.

The version at the Magic Kingdom officially opened in late 1993 (although some sources claim early 1994). The Florida version ended with a final performance August 15, 2006.

At the Magic Kingdom, the Sword in the Stone was staged immediately in front of the Cinderella Carrousel in a small raised area featuring an anvil with the sword firmly imbedded. It required an electronic release from a technician who was located on top of Sir Mickey's shop during the show and who also operated the sound cues.

The premise of the fifteen minute show was that since Good King Arthur was supposedly off on vacation that there was a need for new temporary royal ruler of Fantasyland to "safeguard and protect" the realm in his absence.

Merlin uses his magic including a "locator pigeon" to find the appropriate candidate with no success. Finally, Merlin would pick an adult who despite his best struggles was unable to pull the sword. Then Merlin would select a child who would magically raise the sword half way and be crowned the temporary ruler. The sword only came up half-way because it was felt it was a bad idea for a child to have a heavy dangerous sword to swing.

Unfortunately, it took so long to find the proper ruler that his reign is over so Merlin gave the child a medallion and a certificate.

The text on the approximately eight by ten inch colorful certificate read: 'Walt Disney World. Temporary Ruler of the Realm. Official Certificate of Coronation. Let it be know to one and all that the bearer of this certificate has been duly selected, tested, appointed and has fulfilled their duties as an official temporary Ruler of the Realm. Ceremony presided over and authenticated by Merlin, Court Wizard." It was signed by Merlin with a star instead of a dot over the letter 'i.' The certificate was rolled up and a purple ribbon held it together.

For Walt Disney World, the medallion was roughly an inch and a half in diameter and less than one-fourth of an inch thick. The front of the medallion had a drawing of Wart (young Arthur) from the waist up with an extended left hand pulling the sword up from the rock anvil as he looked up. On the back is a small crown and in fancy script "Temporary Ruler of the Realm' Walt Disney World © Disney." It was attached to a purple lanyard.

After the ceremony, Merlin spent another fifteen minutes signing autographs and greeting guests before he ran backstage to prepare for the next performance.

Mickey's Birthdayland

(1988 - 1990)

Michael Eisner and Frank Wells gave the immediate green light to creating a special land at the Magic Kingdom to celebrate Mickey's special 60th birthday, Mickey's Birthdayland. It was planned to only be there for eighteen months and there was only three months for it to go through the design process after it was approved.

The area allocated included some backstage land near Fantasyland but in addition, the Grand Prix Raceway had to have its track moved and shortened in order to allow for construction of the location.

Brightly colored circus tents seemed very much in keeping with the party spirit and would be easy to erect quickly for the temporary location. Steve Hansen was the show writer and the director for the first new land added to the Magic Kingdom. It was also the smallest land at the Magic Kingdom covering roughly three acres.

The train that circled the park was re-named "Mickey's Birthdayland Express" and was decorated for Mickey's surprise party. Even a new train station was built so that guests could more easily get to the outlying location.

Cindy Williams (of the then popular television program *Laverne & Shirley*) and First Lady Nancy Reagan were on hand to open Mickey's Birthdayland on June 18, 1988.

Where did these Disney toons live? Duckburg! Yes, a town with a population according to the prominent sign of "bill'ions and still growing. A town that's everything it's quacked up to be!" It was just ducky with its quickly built two dimensional storefront facades as primarily photo opportunities leading to the main circus tent. Only Mickey's house was three-dimensional with interior rooms that guests could view.

Why Duckburg, the famed hometown of Donald Duck, Uncle Scrooge and all their friends? The animated syndicated television series *Duck Tales* featuring the adventures of Uncle Scrooge and the nephews in Duckburg had premiered to great success beginning in September 1987.

Mickey's Birthdayland included a children's playground and a topiary/shrub maze. Nearby was Grandma Duck's petting farm filled with goats, pigs, ducks, miniature horses and chickens presented by Friskies. The farm also included Minnie Moo, a white cow that had a black silhouette on one of its sides that looked like Mickey Mouse's head.

Donald Duck had a boat, the S.S. Donald, but it was only a flat façade like ones for the Duckburg News (founded 1928), Scrooge McDuck's Bank, Daisy Duck's Millinery, Goofy's Clip Joint barber shop, HD&L Toys (Huey, Dewey and Louie), Duck County School and more that were on the pathway as photo opportunities.

However, most guests rushed to the Birthday Party Tent. After watching Disney cartoons in the pre-show area, guests could see a live character show called *Minnie's Surprise Party*, celebrating Mickey's birthday. Reportedly, in the beginning, the show would run over two dozen times in a single day.

After the show, guests would proceed to Mickey's dressing room and visit with the birthday boy to get an autograph or a photo. Multiple dressing rooms guaranteed that guests would not be disappointed and that the line would move quickly even with just a small number of guests being allowed to visit at a time.

The area was so popular that instead of closing after eighteen months, it remained open until April 22, 1990 and only closed at that time so the area could be re-themed as Mickey's Starland that opened on May 26, 1990, since the birthday theme was no longer appropriate and the place was, after all, the home of all the Disney cartoon stars.

Mickey's Toontown Fair
(1996 – 2011)

To update the area for Walt Disney World's 25th anniversary in 1996, Mickey's Starland became the more elaborate Mickey's Toontown Fair with three-dimensional additions, taking inspiration from Disneyland's popular Toontown. It officially opened October 1, 1996. It closed in February 2011 to make room for Storybook Circus.

While Mickey and the gang lived in Toontown in Disneyland, this land would be their vacation home on the east coast. One of the reasons they were all taking a vacation was it was the time of year for the big Fair and traditionally Mickey was one of the judges. Mickey takes such pride in being a judge that he appears that way on the entrance sign to the land and his outfit is hung with care in his house.

It is only a temporary Fair because of all the banners that decorate the more permanent structures and the temporary tents that have been erected as well as the temporary sign on the train station. The small land was filled with cartoony details and references to Disney animated shorts.

Pete's Service Station was at the entrance because it is a stereotype that such out-of-the-way service stations would take advantage of unsuspecting and vulnerable tourists, so that is why a Disney villain is running the place. Pete was selling "Gulp" Gas as an homage to "Gulf" gas that was a long time Disney sponsor.

Goofy took over the area of Grandma Duck's farm, but his Wise Acres Farm (a "wise acre" being a slang term for a smart aleck) isn't as successful at farming since his squash has actually been squashed by his big feet and the Goofy scarecrow seems to attract crows.

So, Goofy has tried to survive by crop dusting, although his plane has crashed into the water tower. Guests could board the child-friendly Barnstormer ride on a modified bi-plane for a mild roller-coaster two-minute trip through his farm.

Mickey's Country House gave a glimpse into the home life of the famous star with a view of his bedroom, living room, game room and his kitchen being renovated by Donald Duck and Goofy. The backyard had a path that led by Pluto's doghouse and through Mickey's garage with his workshop, complete with a "Last Aid" kit and "Craftsmouse" tools. An alternative path took guests into the Judge's Tent for a meet-and-greet with a costumed Mickey Mouse.

Minnie's pink and lavender Country House decorated with hearts and flowers allowed guests to visit her living room, interactive kitchen including a quick rising cake in the oven, and her arts and craft studio where she paints, sews and makes pottery. Guests could hear messages on her answering machine. In her backyard was a pink gazebo.

Donald Duck's Boat, the Miss Daisy, is docked in Toon Lake that allowed guests to play in the water that spurted from a spongy foundation. Inside, guests could ring the bell, pull the whistle (that caused water to spout out of the top of the boat) steer the ship, climb on a rope ladder and more. Across from it was Toon Park with slides and other things for very young children.

The big tent housed the County Bounty one of the largest gift shops on property selling souvenirs and the Hall of Fame where guests could meet characters like the Disney princesses (who first debuted there in 2004) or Tinker Bell and her friends in Pixie Hollow. The open-air Toontown Farmer's Market sold fresh fruit, snacks and beverages.

Cornelius Coot

(1988 -2011)

From Mickey's Birthdayland that opened on June 18, 1988 until Mickey's Toontown Fair closed completely in February 2011 for the construction of New Fantasyland, one of the few prominent elements that remained the same was the statue of Cornelius Coot.

Cornelius was a character created by fabled comic book legend Carl Barks for the Donald Duck family stories he was doing for the Disney comic books being published by Dell.

In keeping with the history that Barks had created for Duckburg where the Disney ducks lived, there was a statue of Cornelius Coot, the founder of Duckburg. He was Donald Duck's great-great-grandfather and supposedly scared off Spanish soldiers who were attacking Fort Duckburg by popping corn to fool them into thinking reinforcements had arrived and were firing off their guns.

Coot also piped mountain water into the area that allowed corn crops to flourish and allowed the community of Duckburg to be established. So that is why Coot is proudly holding out an ear of corn and why the statue was in a water fountain.

The statue was an accurate recreation of the one that first appeared in the comic book story "Statuesque Spendthrifts" by Carl Barks in *Walt Disney's Comics and Stories* #138. (March 1952). Afterwards, Coot's statue became a recurring landmark in many comic stories taking place in Duckburg.

The Cornelius Coot statue even made a cameo appearance in the November 1988 episode "Ducks on the Lam" in the *DuckTales* syndicated animated television series.

The statue depicts Cornelius wearing a pilgrim-like hat and fringed shirt. Both of his arms are outstretched and hold ears of corn. The plaque below the statue reads, "This is Old Cornelius

Coot, Who Turned His Corn Crop Into Loot, And Founded Mickey's Toontown Fair, To Him We Dedicate This Square".

Coots are small water birds commonly mistaken to be ducks although there are some significant physical differences.

Why was the statue in Mickey's Birthdayland? Because the land was supposed to be where the Disney toons lived...Duckburg! So, of course, the famous statue needed to be included to identify the location.

The animated syndicated television series Duck Tales, featuring the adventures of Uncle Scrooge and the nephews in Duckburg and inspired by the Barks' comic book stories, had premiered to great success beginning in September 1987.

Show writer for the project Steve Hansen was unfamiliar with any city associated with Mickey Mouse other than Burbank or Hollywood. However, he was a huge fan of Carl Barks' work on his iconic Duck family stories that took place in Duckburg.

The popular film *Who Framed Roger Rabbit* that would make Toontown both the official home for all toons and a place that was readily embraced by the public, would not debut until June 22, 1988 — after the land was built and before the overwhelming success of the film.

Roger Rabbit was quickly shoehorned into the new land as part of the show celebrating Mickey's birthday.

That statue remained when the area became Toontown Fair where Coot was retroactively also made the founder of the Toontown Fair especially since his corn crop fit in nicely with the Fair story of exhibiting prize produce and other blue ribbon winners in the merchandise tent called Cornelius Coot's County Bounty. Supposedly, this iconic treasure is now kept safely in the Disney Archives.

Skyway
(1971 – 1999)

The Disneyland Skyway operated from 1956 to 1994 and Walt Disney called it "a transportation system of the future". It was an opening day attraction at Walt Disney World.

Built by Von Roll of Bern, Switzerland, that had provided similar sky rides for over 100 amusement venues, it offered one-way transportation to Fantasyland or Tomorrowland so it was billed as two separate attractions. No round trips were allowed.

Each colorful, open-aired gondola could hold four adults or roughly 700 pounds. Two guests faced forward and two faced backward as the gondolas lifted up and rocked back and forth on overhead cables for less than five minutes.

The gondolas traveled above the main area of Fantasyland and the crystal clear 20,000 Leagues Under the Sea attraction lagoon provided a wonderful photo opportunity before the vehicles made a sharp right turn near the Tomorrowland Speedway. The journey continued with the gondolas passing Space Mountain before touching down at the Tomorrowland Station.

Guests could even enjoy distant views of the Contemporary Resort, Splash Mountain, and the Grand Floridian Resort and Spa. Pinocchio's Village Haus was designed so that the view looking down from the gondolas mimicked the opening overhead shot of Gepetto's village from the animated feature.

In February 1999, a park custodian at Walt Disney World's Magic Kingdom was killed when the skyway started up expectedly while he was cleaning one of its platforms. Raymond Barlow, 65, was sweeping off a narrow skyway platform inaccessible to park guests an hour after the park's 9:00 A.M. opening when other cast members, unaware of his presence, started up the ride.

Barlow, startled by the approaching gondola, grabbed onto it and tried to climb inside and fell forty feet into a flower bed, hitting a tree on the way down, and died. The Occupational Safety and Health Administration later ruled that the area in which Barlow had been working violated federal safety codes and fined Walt Disney World $4,500 for a "serious" violation of safety standards

The last day of operation for the attraction was in November 1999 because the cost of operating and maintaining the attraction was high in relation to its hourly capacity as well as the need to upgrade it for disabled access and structural repairs. There were also increasing concerns about liability with guests rocking the gondolas, as well as spitting and throwing things out of them onto the guests walking below.

"It's part of our ongoing efforts to phase out some of the older attractions and introduce new things to keep our parks exciting for our new and repeat visitors," Walt Disney World spokesman Diane Ledder told the media. "It's just something whose time has come."

When the Fantasyland Station closed, the pylons and wires were removed from the park, but some of the equipment remained in the building. The Bavarian-style Alpine building that featured a large clock still reflected the village theme of the area. The front area was used for stroller parking.

The station was eventually removed and replaced by the Tangled Restrooms as well as a wider path to Liberty Square.

The Tomorrowland Station was two stories high with a waterfall on one side. When it closed, the top half of the building and the waterfall were eventually removed and a bathroom was installed on the ground floor.

The DisneyStyle store at Disney Springs has a blue Skyway gondola hanging from the ceiling just above the Mad Tea Party teacup photo-op.

Flight to the Moon/ Mission to Mars
(1971 - 1993)

Disneyland opened in July 1955 with an attraction called Rocket to the Moon that simulated a trip around the moon and when the New Tomorrowland debuted in 1967, the attraction was redesigned as Flight to the Moon. This revised version opened at WDW on December 24, 1971.

Inside were two "Lunar Transports" theaters meant to represent the passenger cabins in a space ship. The pre-show allowed guests to see pre-launch activity in Mission Control, "the nerve center of Disneyland's spaceport". Eight audio-animatronics male figures were seated along two banks of computers moving their heads and arms.

The one standing figure who talked to the audience was Control Center Director Mr. Tom Morrow. Screens behind Mr. Morrow showed some NASA footage, new projects that were being prepared and the preparations for Flight 92 (that the guests would soon be boarding for their flight) as well as the famous footage from runway 12 where a clumsy albatross came in for an awkward landing that tripped security alarms.

Once in the theater, the upper ceiling and lower floor projection screens showed some of the same material from the original attraction with flares lighting up the dark side of the moon and being caught in a meteoroid shower on the return to the Earth. However, during the nine minute moon flight, two screens mounted on opposite sides of the cabin's walls showed a new "live" telecast from the moon's surface of astronauts gathering ore samples, demonstrating weightlessness and showing off the nearby moon base.

However, even as it was being installed at WDW, it was obsolete even though publicity stated "Disney called on NASA experts to provide data. The new show is as scientifically authentic, accurate and up-to-date as possible". NASA had purposely withheld information including the actual design of the moon landing vehicle.

In March 1975, the new version entitled Mission to Mars opened but it was not a simple overlay.

The entrance and holding areas were redone. More importantly, a female audio-animatronics character took over one of the seats in the Mission Control pre-show.

Mr. Tom Morrow was replaced by the audio-animatronics bespectacled Mr. Johnson (who was voiced by actor George Walsh who had previously supplied the voice for Mr. Morrow) with his headset and clipboard discussing space travel and the Mars vehicle. The new show included Mars footage shot by a NASA satellite.

Of course, there was no base on Mars for astronauts to transmit a "live" broadcast to the guests. So that section was changed to images from probes launched from the rocket and narrated by Third Officer Collins voiced by Peter Renoudet. Those probes showed details of the surface of the planet including canyons and mountains.

Some things that had delighted guests in the previous show remained including the footage of the albatross tripping the security alarms and the danger from a meteoroid shower forcing the ship's immediate return to earth.

The theaters remained the same as earlier incarnation with four tiers and screens on the top and bottom. However, when the moon came into view, the ship jumped into "hyper-space penetration" that brought Mars into range.

Some guests had lost interest in real space flights so weren't as interested in this new destination adventure and attendance quickly dwindled and was closed in October 1993. The ExtraTERRORestrial Alien Encounter opened in the space June 1995.

ExtraTERRORestrial Alien Encounter

(1995 – 2003)

ExtraTERRORestrial Alien Encounter opened in Tomorrowland in June 1995, replacing the Mission to Mars attraction. It was originally intended as an attraction for the never produced Tomorrowland 2055 make-over at Disneyland and would have been based on the *Alien* movie franchise that began in 1979.

Filmmaker George Lucas was brought in to work on the concept and abandoned any connection to the *Alien* movie franchise because it was determined to be too traumatic and intense for Disney guests.

Despite the word "terror" being in all capital letters as the name of the attraction and the many warning signs that stated that it was " a frightening theatrical experience in a confined setting with loud noises and moments of total darkness (that) may be too intense for children and some adults", guests were still unprepared for the sensory experience that was finally presented and there were complaints.

Guests entered the Tomorrowland Interplanetary Convention Center to witness a demonstration of the alien corporation X-S Tech's latest technological innovation. The lobby show music consisted of twelve original musical selections composed specifically for the attraction by George Wilkins as well as posters and videos that humorously referenced Disney related science-fiction efforts including "Lunar Disneyland. The Happiest Place Off Earth".

Chairman L.C. Clench (actor Jeffrey Jones) who was excited to find a new world to sell his products told the guests, "If something can't be done with X-S (Excess), then it shouldn't be done at all!"

In the pre-show, the amoral robot S.I.R. (Simulated Intelligence Robotics), voiced by Tim Curry gave a disturbing demonstration of the newest Series 1000 teleportation device as he transports the adorable alien Skippy across the room where he reappears burnt, in pain, scared and confused.

Guests proceeded to an amphitheater Testing Center of concentric circles of seating surrounding a large cylindrical teleportation tube similar to the one they had just seen in the pre-show. For "safety reasons", each seat included gigantic over the shoulder harnesses that locked down on each guest.

Binaural audio like the breathing of the alien would be pumped through two special speakers located next to each ear along with warm, moist water (to simulate the creature's drool and the blood of a killed technician and exploded alien) and hot air effects (to simulate the creature's tongue licking the guest's head). The feeling of being restrained added to the anxiety of being in the dark.

Clench decides to use the device to teleport himself to the audience but something in the signal path intercepts the transmission. What appears in the tube is not Clench but an extraterrestrial that is tall with spider-like legs, gnashing fangs, glowing red eyes and transparent wings. It is determined to be carnivorous.

It crashes through the tube and the theater goes dark and the audience imagines this creature right behind them. The alien is lured back into the tube and exploded.

The attraction closed in 2003 and was replaced by a similar but more comical and family-friendly attraction called Stitch's Great Escape in 2004. The Interplanetary Convention Center was recast as the Galactic Federation Prisoner Transport Center, with guests recruited as trainees in the cosmic government's justice system and witnessing the arrival of a Level 3 prisoner, Stitch, who escapes into the WDW park.

That attraction went to seasonal-only operation in 2016 and is now permanently closed.

Diamond Horseshoe Revue

(1971 – 1986)

The Golden Horseshoe Revue was a popular musical entertainment attraction and food and beverage location in Frontierland at Disneyland that premiered opening day in 1955. The music for the show including *"Hello, Everybody!"* was written by Charles LaVere, who served as the show's original pianist, and had lyrics by Tom Adair. The script for the production was co-authored by two of its stars, Wally Boag and Donald Novis.

A duplicate of the show called the *Diamond Horseshoe Revue* directed by Boag opened in Frontierland at Walt Disney World on opening day in 1971. The park brochure described it as "A rollicking stage show right out of the Old West featuring a cast of dancing girls, comedians and singers including Slue Foot Sue herself."

It ran until October 1, 1986 when it became the *Diamond Horseshoe Jamboree* with Sam the bartender and Miss Lilly that ran until 1995. Several other shows and food service options occupied the location until it became a seasonal only venue.

The interior of the traditional circa 1860 saloon featured a raised stage for the performers with a small three piece band on the floor in front of it. There were round tables and wooden chairs on the main floor for guests with seating also available in a horseshoe-shaped balcony area.

While the show was free, because of limited seating of less than a thousand guests a day even with multiple shows, tickets had to be obtained early in the morning at the hospitality desk located in Main Street's Town Square.

Guests could purchase soft drinks, cold sandwiches and chips. The income from the food service rarely covered the cost of the labor, much less the performers which was one of the reasons for the show closing. It lasted as long as it did because it was a favorite show of Dick Nunis who ran the parks. The show was sponsored by Del Monte from 1979 -1984.

Other than being larger physically, the only major change in the Diamond Horseshoe was that the bar was located on the left side of the room rather than the right as in Disneyland. When Boag returned to California late in 1973, he was replaced by Bert Henry who had been replacing him at Disneyland.

The roughly thirty-minute show always played to full audiences. Owner Slue Foot Sue and her four dancing girls welcomed the audience in song. She later introduced the emcee and Irish tenor who sang a song. A comedic traveling salesman did a comedy routine that included making balloon animals.

Sue and the emcee sang the song "Pecos Bill" from the Disney animated featurette and were interrupted by the re-appearance of the traveling salesman now attired as the iconic cowboy of folklore. One of the memorable moments was Pecos Bill being accidentally hit in the face and spitting out his "teeth" at the audience. The finale featured Sue's girls doing a can-can dance and the entire company in a final song.

On August 1986, Dennis Despie, vice president of entertainment for Disneyland and Walt Disney World said about the show closing, "We all recognize the revue at the Golden Horseshoe and Diamond Horseshoe Saloon as one of the most enduring shows in the history of the park. At the same time, we feel we should now develop a new generation of shows."

The only vintage items of the Walt Disney World version of the show were postcards and a Pana-vue slide. A limited edition pin was produced many years later.

McDonalds Fry Cart

(1999 – 2007)

McDonald's executive Ray Kroc wrote the following letter to Walt Disney on October 20, 1954:

> Dear Walt, I feel somewhat presumptuous addressing you in this way yet I feel sure you would not want me to address you any other way. My name is Ray A. Kroc....I look over the Company A picture we had taken at Sound Beach, Conn., many times and recall a lot of pleasant memories...I have very recently taken over the national franchise of the McDonald's system. I would like to inquire if there may be an opportunity for a McDonald's in your Disneyland Development.

Walt was assigned to the American Red Cross Ambulance Corps unit training in Sound Beach in 1918 and Kroc was also in that unit. Kroc claimed he never received a response from Disneyland manager C.V. Wood to whom Walt forwarded the request.

McDonald's did get a presence in Disney theme parks due to an agreement with Disney from 1997 to 2007.

The McDonald's Fry Cart that opened in 1999 was located near Pecos Bill's Tall Tale Inn and Café and sold its famous French fries and soft drinks. Disney Imagineers wrote the following back story for that location:

With the rush of prospectors passing through Frontierland in search of gold, lots of folks in town started looking for ways to cash in on all the excitement. Back in 1853, ol' McDonald (who had a farm, "ei-ei-o"), a potato farmer, decided to set up his cook wagon on the hill under the big oak tree, just off the main trail.

To drum up interest in his French fried delicacies, McDonald even came up with a catch phrase and posted it on the front of the wagon: "There's gold in them thar fries!" (with a symbol of a golden arch to emphasize the fact).

Business was booming for a couple of good years, right up until the great flood of 1855. Legend has it that white men disturbed the spirits of the mountain by removing gold from Big Thunder, causing all sorts of havoc from earthquakes and avalanches to storms and floods.

In fact, the nearby river rose so much, the water reached right up to McDonald's wagon on the hill. The wagon survived, but when the water receded, the wagon started to go with it. It slid down the hill, crashed through a fence (and sharp-eyed guests could see the poorly repaired fence and a broken wagon wheel), and got lodged in the mud down below.

This didn't stop ol' man McDonald, though. He just laid down some planks so folks wouldn't get their boots muddy, and he has kept right on selling his delicious French fried potatoes until the Disney agreement ended.

There was also a sign placed nearby that proclaimed, "Same location since '53." The "53" was scratched out and painted over with a "55." Not only did this help support the story that the wagon had moved, it was also a reference to McDonald's history.

Brothers Dick and Mac McDonald opened their original restaurant in San Bernardino, California, in 1953. Kroc, who pitched the idea to the brothers of expanding their restaurant into a franchise, opened his first location in Des Plaines, Illinois in 1955.

The Frontierland Fry Cart closed in December 2007.

The Golden Oak Outpost opened in the location on January 11, 2009. The name is a tribute to Disney's Golden Oak Ranch in California, an 800-acre movie ranch where Disney filmed a great many live-action television shows and films.

The Enchanted Tiki Room
Under New Management
(1998 – 2011)

The Enchanted Tiki Room Under New Management ran at Magic Kingdom's Adventureland after a seven month transformation of the original version from April 1998 to January 2011.

"The new management" were audio-animatronics figures of Iago (voiced by Gilbert Gottfried) from the animated feature *Aladdin* and Zazu (voiced by Michael Gough rather than the film's Rowan Atkinson) from the animated feature *The Lion King* who had "been given the deed to the WDW Tiki Room as part of their bonuses for starring in hit movies as negotiated by their agents William and Morris (voiced by Don Rickles and Phil Hartman)".

In particular, Iago sought to update the show and make it more hip for a modern audience but his approach is cynical and jarring and angers Uh-Oa, the green audio-animatronics "Tiki Goddess of Disaster" (voiced by Armelia Audrey McQueen) who emerges in smoke from the center fountain to punish him.

Iago later appears at the end of the show bandaged, burnt and with a crutch but not humbled by the experience. The revamped show was done by senior concept designer Jeff Burke and senior concept writer Kevin Rafferty.

"It was kind of demoralizing to see guests leave in the middle of the (original) show," said Burke. "So we wanted to infuse new life into it. We wanted to bring out the Disney magic that current audiences would relate to. People who have seen the show before will wonder 'What is going on around here?'"

For the recording session, three of the four original voices for the Tiki Bird hosts were brought back: Wally Boag (Jose), Fulton Burley (Michael), and Thurl Ravenscroft (Fritz). Ernie Newton who did Pierre had passed away in 1996 and was replaced by Jerry Orbach.

Associate show producer Kate Zovich took pride in the creation of the two new audio-animatronics characters, "The work that (Imagineering in) Tujunga (California) did on the A-A figures is absolutely amazing. To fit all of that wiring and mechanics inside these teeny birds is an incredible accomplishment and they were very successful at making these figures more like cartoon characters."

Most guests were appalled that the lighthearted original show had been replaced by the newer snarkier version that eliminated familiar songs and had too many in-jokes like Iago commenting at the end of the show, "Boy, I'm tired! I think I'll head over to the Hall of Presidents and take a nap."

While curious enough to visit, guests were generally displeased with the misguided attempts at humor so they didn't revisit, defeating the purpose for the drastic changes.

On January 12, 2011, a small fire broke out in the attic of the attraction, damaging the figure of Iago as well as other show elements when the automatic sprinkler system went off to extinguish the flames.

The decision was made to replace the show with a newly shortened version of the original show now dubbed Walt Disney's Enchanted Tiki Room that opened August 15, 2011.

However, a reminder of the ill-fated new management attraction exists at Trader Sam's Grog Grotto in the Polynesian Village Resort. One of its signature drinks is the Uh-Oa. Above the bar is the Uh-Oa goddess figure from the attraction. If a guest orders the drink, a storm begins outside with winds and heavy rains.

The bartenders lead guests in the chant of "Uh-Oa, Uh-Oa, Uh Oa-aaaa!" and the Krakatoa volcano erupts and ligthning flashes illuminate the goddess figure who opens her eyes to reveal their glowing redness and she cackles, just as she did in the attraction.

Muppets Liberty Square

(2016 – 2019)

Disney acquired the rights to Jim Henson's Muppets in February 2004 and tried to reboot the franchise starting in 2008 with new movies and television appearances. Henson had entered into negotiations with the Disney company for the franchise before his death in 1990 resulting in the characters being incorporated into shows at Disney MGM Studios.

However, after Henson's death, Disney was unable to finalize the acquistion from the Henson family but were able to arrange a license for the Muppet*Vision 3-D attraction. With Disney's purchase in 2004 the word "Muppet" became a Disney trademark.

After the release of the theaterical feature film *Muppets Most Wanted* (2014), Disney decided to develop a theme park show about American history that would have featured Sam Eagle interacting with guests and telling in typical Muppet fashion an unintentionally humorous version of famous events where he gets the stories partially right and mostly wrong.

Jim Lewis who had written extensively for The Muppets for thirty years was brought in for consultation and the show expanded to include Kermit, Miss Piggy, Fozzie Bear, Gonzo and two of Gonzo's chicken friends. James Silson and Tara Anderson were co-directors of the show. Brendan Milburn and Valerie Vigoda wrote a new song for the shows.

The Muppets Present...Great Moments in American History premiered in Liberty Square at the Magic Kingdom on October 2, 2016 with two different shows, The Declaration of Independence and The Midnight Ride of Paul Revere. The Muppets perform in the upper three windows above the Heritage House gift shop so that it appears as if it is three interconnected television screens.

Because of the distance to the guests below, the puppets were made about five percent larger than the traditional Muppets and were built by the same craftspeople who build the characters for television and film. The pre-recorded voices were provided by Steve Whitmire (Kermit the Frog), Eric Jacobson (Miss Piggy, Fozzie Bear, Sam Eagle) and Dave Goelz (Gonzo) and the Muppets' actions are synchronized by live puppeteers to that voice track.

The puppeteers are also responsible for several costume changes during the show. Each show lasted approximately ten minutes and were performed multiple times during the day.

The Declaration of Independence show has Sam appearing in a circular portal at the top of the Hall of Presidents and interacting with a live James Jefferson (aka "JJ"), the Town Crier of Liberty Square down below who leads the guests in different responses during the show. As they attempt to share the events surrounding the drafting of the famous document, the other Muppets appear in the Heritage House windows.

These other Muppets portray historical figures Thomas Jefferson (Kermit), John Adams (Gonzo) and Benjamin Franklin (Fozzie). Miss Piggy is irritated that there are no female roles and decides to change King George III and later George Washington into "Georgette" for her to perform as those characters.

Midnight Ride of Paul Revere takes place solely in the windows above Heritage House and is a very loose adaptation of Henry Wadsworth Longfellow's famous poem Paul Revere's Ride. Kermit portrays Revere and has a stick horse whose face surprisingly animates as another Muppet.

"The show really appeals to everybody, across generations, because the Muppets have such a wonderful history," said Tara Anderson. "Parents are going to watch the show with their children and they're both going to laugh! It's the Muppets we know and love, but new."

Main Street Electrical Parade

The iconic Main Street Electrical Parade (MSEP) "glowed away" for a final time October 9, 2016.

The Main Street Electrical Parade was created as a night time experience for Disneyland in 1972 and then cloned for WDW and debuted June 11, 1977. However, after that date, the WDW version of the Main Street Electrical Parade had a pretty convoluted history.

At WDW, it continued to entertain guests until its final show on September 14, 1992. It was replaced by SpectroMagic until 1999.

After closing at Disneyland in 1996 (and replaced by Light Magic in 1997), the Disneyland version of the parade known as the "crown jewel of summer" underwent a dazzling makeover of 575,000 glittering new lights.

In May 1999, the parade returned back to Walt Disney World as part of WDW's Millennium Celebration where it continued to entertain guests until April 1, 2001 after more than 500 performances.

The parade went to Disney's California Adventure to try to brighten that struggling park's attendance. Walt Disney World re-introduced SpectroMagic as the nighttime parade.

On June 6, 2010, MSEP once again returned to the Magic Kingdom for a supposedly limited engagement just that summer as part of the *Summer Nightastic!* promotion event but was so popular that it was extended until October 2016.

When Walt Disney World opened in 1971, the Seven Seas Lagoon was dark and forbidding at night. As a backdrop for the South Seas Luau to lighten things up, the Electrical Water Pageant was created as a temporary solution.

It premiered "officially" at a nighttime press event luau on the shore of the Polynesian Village Resort on Sunday, October 24 as part of the three day weekend dedication festivities of Walt Disney World.

It was a reasonably simple and inexpensive option. Several floating barges were pulled across the lagoon by a boat. On each barge was a flat, framed, twenty-five foot tall, wire screen decorated with Christmas tree lights powered by a noisy generator that couldn't be heard out on the water in the distance. A sea serpent, a whale, jumping dolphins, seahorses and even King Neptune frolicked on the man-made body of water.

A special version of Gershon Kingsley & Jean Jeaque Perrey's 1967 composition "Baroque Hoedown" was created specifically for the Electrical Water Pageant and then later adapted for the MSEP.

With all the Disney Company emphasis on Walt Disney World, Disneyland was being neglected so Disney Company President Card Walker wanted something to entice guests to stay later in the park and buy more souvenirs and food.

The delight of the Electrical Water Pageant inspired the MSEP and the first floats were similar by being flat two-dimensional screens with simple lights. Bob Jani and Ron Miziker are given the official credit by the Disney Company for being the creators and producers of the original MSEP. Jani had supervised the creation of the Electrical Water Pageant.

Miziker had done some research that with the introduction of electricity, local Main Streets in the United States would hold nighttime parades with strings of lights stretched over the street.

Since Disneyland had its own turn of the century Main Street, a parade with lights seemed a natural and the continuing success of the Electrical Water Pageant showed how the parade could be accomplished. Basically, it was felt that all they needed to do was put wheels on the barges. However, the parade evolved into something much more elaborate and innovative before its June debut.

Magic Kingdom Parades

At a Disney theme park, every day is a special occasion. Originally, the idea of a parade was to provide a free entertainment experience for a large number of guests without needing a stage facility.

The Magic Kingdom was the first Disney park that had a planned parade route. A dedicated facility for the floats and performers was built behind where the Splash Mountain attraction is today. A circular pathway was created so the vehicles could easily access the entrance gates by the Car Barn on Main Street to either start the parade or finish the parade and be able to return to the backstage facility with ease.

Sophisticated sound systems are located behind some of the upper floor Main Street USA windows that open during the parade. Both America on Parade and the Main Street Electrical Parade prompted breakthroughs in parade technology of using sound, float engineering, costuming, logistics and more that are still the foundation for today's Walt Disney World parades.

America on Parade (1975-1976): This parade celebrated America's bicentennial at both Walt Disney World and Disneyland. At the time, this parade was Disney's largest, with more than 150 performers and about 50 unique floats representing key moments in America's history, as well as cultural aspects like picnics in the park. A few Disney characters made appearances towards the end representing American films and television. The Sherman Brothers wrote a special song for the parade.

Share A Dream Come True/Dreams Come True/Celebrate a Dream Come True Parade (2001 – 2014): Originally in celebration of Walt Disney's 100th Birthday, this parade featured giant snow globe floats and included Walt Disney World's first interactive performance parade stop. However, it was quickly realized that the snow globes did not have proper ventilation for the performers so they had to be redesigned.

The floats featured the following themes: "It Was All Started By A Mouse" (Mickey Mouse), "Wish Upon A Star" (Pinocchio), "A Thousand Dreams To See" (Aladdin), "Face The Darkest Fears" (Disney Villains), "A Dream is a Wish Your Heart Makes" (Princes and Princess) and "As Long as There is Imagination Left in the World" (assorted characters). In 2006, the parade changed its name and some elements. It was renamed again in 2009.

A listing of some of the MK parades:

- Character Parade/Cavalcade of Characters (1971-1975, 1977-1978)
- Mickey's 50th Birthday Parade (1978)
- Dumbo's Circus Parade (1979)
- Walt Disney World's Tencennial Parade (1981-1982)
- Mickey Mouse Character Parade (1983)
- Donald's 50th Birthday Parade (1984)
- Mickey's Street Party (1985 -1986)
- Walt Disney World's 15th Anniversary Parade (1986)
- Spirit of America (1987-1988)
- Mickey's All American Birthday Parade (1988 -1990)
- Disney's Character Hit Parade/Zip Parade (1989 – 1991)
- Walt Disney World's 20th Anniversary "Surprise" Celebration Parade (1991 – 1994)
- Mickey Mania Parade (1994 – 1996)
- Walt Disney World's 25th Anniversary "Remember the Magic" Parade (1996 – 1997)
- Magical Moments Parade Parade (1998 – 2001)
- Happy Easter Parade (1972 – 1998)
- Mickey's Very Merry Christmas Parade/ Mickey's Once Upon a Christmastime Parade (1978 – present)
- Mickey's Not So Scary Halloween Parade/ Mickey's Boo to You Parade (1997- present)
- Main Street Trolley Parade (February 2003 – present)
- Main Street Electrical Parade (1977–1991, 1999–2001, 2010–2016)
- SpectroMagic! (1991–1999, 2001–2010)

Splash Mountain

The Walt Disney Company announced in June 2020 that it would be immediately re-theming Splash Mountain to the animated feature film *The Princess and the Frog* (2009).

Splash Mountain opened at Disneyland on July 17, 1989 and three years later on July 17, 1992 at Walt Disney World's Magic Kingdom as well as Tokyo Disneyland that same year.

Splash Mountain was created at Disneyland for three business reasons. First, Executive Vice President Dick Nunis wanted a water flume ride at the park. Second, a big attraction was needed to draw more attendance to the dead end cul-de-sac known as Bear Country. Third, the America Sings attraction was closing and this was an opportunity to re-use the audio-animatronics.

Imagineer Tony Baxter found the solution to all three challenges with the idea that it could all be themed to the Disney feature film *Song of the South* (1946), especially since the audio-animatronics characters had been designed by Marc Davis who had animated similar characters for the problematic film.

At one point, CEO Michael Eisner looked at the model and said, "It's a mountain ... you have a big splash at the end ... it's Splash Mountain."

At Eisner's insistence, Uncle Remus would not be shown or mentioned in the attraction for fear of possible controversy. In fact, the ride would just reflect the three animated segments in the film and ignore the live action story and characters.

The attraction loosely follows some of the incidents in the animated sections of the *Song of the South* film. Brer Rabbit runs away from home and finds himself in more adventures than he intended. He continually outwits Brer Fox and Brer Bear until he is trapped in honey (rather than the politically incorrect Tar Baby in the movie) and taken to Brer Fox's lair to be eaten.

As in the movie, he convinces Brer Fox to toss him into the spiky Briar Patch, where the plucky rabbit survives because he was born and bred in it. The grand finale has the Oscar-winning "Zip a Dee Doo Dah" song being sung by critters on a massive rocking showboat, one of the few things not sculpted out of cement to prevent water damage.

At Walt Disney World, the project was turned over to an entirely different team of Imagineers led by Eric Jacobson. There had to be some significant exterior color changes to blend into the Frontierland color scheme (rather than the Georgia-looking red coloring at Disneyland). The ride and the queue are both longer than at Disneyland.

At Walt Disney World, there is a stronger presence of Brer Frog (Uncle Remus' fishing buddy in the original movie) as a storyteller. The ride vehicles were designed so that guests could ride side-by-side rather than Disneyland's sitting in a single file like the original Matterhorn bobsleds.

There are significantly more audio-animatronics characters in the Disneyland version because they were rescued from America Sings. In Florida, there are fewer such figures because they were expensive to build.

A favorite Florida addition is the weasel located in the cavern scene, the last scene before the water log reaches the incline for the big drop. He pops out of the ceiling when the water log is approaching Brer Fox and Brer Rabbit,

He shouts "FSU" (Florida State University), although is sounds somewhat like a sneeze, because one of the Imagineers was a graduate of that school. Interestingly, this character was also included in the Tokyo Disneyland version.

Of course, the cost of converting this attraction into Princess Tiana after the magical kiss celebrating Mardi Gras with Lou the trumpet-playing alligator means that something else will not get built or fixed.

Epcot

Epcot, originally called Epcot Center, opened October 1, 1982 and was divided into Future World and World Showcase. During its years of operation, it has constantly undergone transformation and re-branding with the current attempt changing the park into four "neighborhoods": World Celebration, World Nature, World Discovery and World Showcase.

Not only is it challenging to try to document the major changes at the park over the decades but often forgotten are the smaller items that delighted guests but were also removed during all the changes like the following:

For some guests, a favorite memory was hearing from 1986 to 1994, the song *Tomorrow's Child* in the finale of the Spaceship Earth attraction that was composed by Peter Stougaard and Ron Ovadia and sung by soloist Sally Stevens.

For over ten years, six double deck buses built on a Chevrolet truck chassis operated at the park. Originally, they were filled with guests and journeyed slowly around World Showcase Promenade with stops at Norway, Italy, France, and Canada. The park did not list them as an attraction but as a "service" and a klaxon horn was sounded to try to get oblivious guests in front of them out of the way.

One bus was later decorated as a Junkanoo Bus Show for four years. Another was formatted with luggage, international flags and Mickey glove hubcaps as part of "Characters on Holiday" for character meet-and-greet opportunities.

Until 2014, the World Showcase Players, an improvisation group of performers, entertained guests in the United Kingdom and Italy pavilions often by pulling in guests to participate in their twenty minute storytelling of "Arthur's Quest for the Holy Grail" and "Romeo and Edna".

That same year, Epcot eliminated other entertainment acts including Off Kilter, the rock band in the Canada pavilion,

Mo'Rockin', a musical ensemble in Morocco and The Spirit of America Fife & Drum Corps that marched in front of the American Adventure attraction.

The boat ride called "Listen to the Land" that drifted through the four greenhouses was transformed with some significant updates into "Living with the Land" in December 1993. Harvest Theater was home to the film *Symbiosis* until 1995 when it was replaced by "Circle of Life: An Environmental Fable".

Designed to celebrate the new century, the sixty thousand square foot Millennium Village (October 1999 to January 1, 2001) included representations from several countries not already part of the World Showcase including exhibits from Brazil, Chile, Eritrea, Israel, Saudi Arabia, Scotland and Sweden. The location also included an international food court with eight regional kitchens, artisans from seven different countries demonstrating their work and the 250 seat World Showplace Theater for performances.

When The Living Seas pavilion became The Seas With Nemo and Friends in 2006, guests saw the loss of the infamous Hydrolators that transported up to thirty guests at a time to and from Sea Base Alpha at the "bottom of the sea".

At one time, three water fountains "talked" to guests with a variety of responses. One was outside Mouse Gear, another to the right of the children play fountain before the bridge to World Showcase and finally one behind Innoventions West near the restroom. There was a talking trashcan inside the Electric Umbrella restaurant that was triggered to talk when trash was put inside it, although there is some question whether it might return after that location has been refurbished even though the talking water fountains did not.

Mickey's Wand
(2000 – 2007)

The Walt Disney Company continually struggled to create a brand identity for Epcot that would be appealing to guests. At one time, it publicized Epcot as the "Discovery Park".

As part of the Millenium Celebration in 2000, Disney installed a twenty-five story high "magic wand" held by Mickey Mouse's hand next to the Spaceship Earth sphere. Mickey's arm was meant to suggest his appearance in the "Sorcerer Apprentice" sequence of the animated feature *Fantasia* (1940). However, in that film, Mickey never used a magic wand but a mystical hat belonging to the wizard Yensid.

At the top of the sphere was a large "2000" number decorated with glittery "starfetti". In 2001, the number was replaced with the word "Epcot". The wand structure had cost more than the Cinderella Castle Cake makeover for the 25th anniversary of the Magic Kingdom. It was too expensive to take down especially when AT&T decided to leave as a sponsor for the attraction and wouldn't assist with the cost of removal as it had for the installation.

So rather than having to spend money each year to change the year number, it was easier to just change the sign to "Epcot" in a script font different from the park's official logo. The steel structure still weighed 500,000 pounds and extended 257 feet -- the tallest theme park structure at Walt Disney World Resort at the time.

According to Roger Holzberg, a senior show producer with Walt Disney Imagineering (WDI), the intent of the icon design was "to wed a core Disney element -- the Sorcerer Mickey hand and wand -- with the futuristic vision of Spaceship Earth in an effort to better identify the spherical entryway to Epcot" that was considered "too plain" for modern guests.

A Walt Disney World press release in December 2000 proudly announced, "The makeover will turn the 15-month Walt Disney World Millennium Celebration icon created for Spaceship Earth into a new and lasting beacon to a magical Disney world." In actuality, the addition seemed to diminish the size of the simple and elegant sphere structure.

Disney released the following numbers about the new icon:

- 257 feet: Height to the sparkles above the tip of Sorcerer Mickey's wand

- 250 tons: Weight of steel frame supporting the icon

- 100,000 pounds: Weight of Mickey's gloved hand, the wand and the "Epcot" lettering

- 250,000: Number of shimmering metallic eye-catchers used to spell "Epcot"

- 36 feet: Height of the tallest letters in "Epcot"

- 5 months: Duration of the construction changeover from "2000" to "Epcot"

On July 5, 2007, Epcot Vice President Jim MacPhee announced that Spaceship Earth would be restored to its original appearance, and that the "magic wand" structure would be removed in time for the park's 25th anniversary on October 1, 2007.

It was rumored that Siemens AG, the new sponsor of Spaceship Earth, requested the wand be removed as it did not fit their corporate image and assisted in the cost. The attraction was closed on July 9, 2007, and by October 1 the wand structure, the stars and their supports were gone.

The structure was cantilevered over Spaceship Earth, so care had to be taken to avoid having it crash through the structure of the sphere building. Workers removed pieces one by one, as if dismantling a giant erector set structure.

A "Spaceship Earth wand reflector part" was offered for auction on Ebay. The winning bidder bought the reflector part for $202.50 and $3.00 for shipping.

CommuniCore

(1982 – 1994)

Disney described CommuniCore as "Future World's global Main Street of ideas and inventions". CommuniCore was located in two crescent-shaped, 100,000 square foot buildings (CommuniCore East and CommuniCore West) that circled a large fountain just beyond Spaceship Earth.

The name was a combination of the words "community" and "core". CommuniCore was meant to provide guests with an introduction and more information about the park's major themes in a somewhat tranquil setting. It was supposed to embody Walt Disney's original plan for Epcot to be a community with a core of information. The logo for CommuniCore was two crescent shapes facing each other divided into north and south quadrants.

The buildings housed rotating exhibits related to technology and were replaced in 1994 by Innoventions which was a combination of the words "innovation" and "inventions". The new area was louder and flashier with more upscale corporate-sponsored exhibits that continued to change.

CommuniCore had a central, tall, winding corridor that ran though each of the buildings from end to end, with a number of entry/exit points to the outside.

CommuniCore officially included the largest shop in Epcot, the two-story 13,000 square foot Centorium (an Emporium for the 21st Century). It also included two restaurants, the Stargate Restaurant (that later became the Electric Umbrella) and Sunrise Terrace Restaurant (that later became Pasta Piazza and Fountainview Expresso & Bakery) that were both open for breakfast, lunch and dinner.

- **CommuniCore East** showcased the Astuter Computer Revue (later Backstage Magic) demonstrating the use of computers at the park and SMRT-1 (Smart One) a purple and chrome robot sitting on a revolving pedestal surrounded by telephones who played games using voice recognition technology with the guests and both exhibits sponsored by Sperry/UNISYS; *Compute-A-Coaster* where guests could assemble their own roller coaster on a video screen with assistance from an animated beaver; American Express' Travelport, a fourteen foot red sphere showing different vacation destinations as well as a Travel Service desk to make plans for a trip; Exxon's Energy Exchange with games, demonstrations, films and interactive experiences like generating enough electricity for a light bulb and getting the optimum gas mileage from a car; and the Electronic Forum which had the Future Choice Theater registering guests' opinions on a variety of topics.

- **CommuniCore West** showcased a communications themed area sponsored by AT&T called FutureCom that predicted services that would be provided by the internet; ExpoRobotics with exhibits on precision maneuvering like painting by industrial robot arms was first on display at the 1985 International Science Exposition in Takuba, Japan but purchased from the manufacturers by WDW; the EPCOT Discovery Center, a research center all about E.P.C.O.T. Center and Walt Disney World (later called "Ask EPCOT" and finally EPCOT Outreach); and a Teacher Center.

CommuniCore was packed with many other displays including the Population clock that displayed the rough population of the Earth and changed with every passing second as well as the Manufactory where guests could assemble an American flag.

Just outside of CommuniCore was the WorldKey Information System kiosks, a digital information system created specifically for Epcot by Bell Laboratories and Western Electric. The main station was in the post-show area outside of Spaceship Earth until 1994. By accessing the touch screen, guests could learn about different attractions and connect with Guest Relations cast members via closed circuit video for assistance or make dining reservations.

Actor Dallas McKennon known for providing the old prospector safety spiel on Big Thunder Mountain Railroad and the voice of Benjamin Franklin in the American Adventure provided the host voice for the kiosks.

Astuter Computer Revue
(1982 -1984)

In 1969, an RCA press release stated that for their planned involvement in the Walt Disney World project the "focal point of WEDCOMM (Walter E. Disney Communications Oriented Monitoring and Management System) would be the RCA System Communication Center, open to the public as a highlight of the Tomorrowland area of the new Theme Park."

To help WDW guests understand about computers, RCA was going to produce a show designed by Imagineer John Hench tentatively titled *Alice in Computer Land*. However when RCA sold its computer division to Sperry Univac (which later became UNISYS), RCA decided to sponsor a different attraction, Space Mountain.

Sperry Univac went on to sponsor another attraction based on a revised version of Hench's concept that would help WDW guests understand about the use of computers to run the Walt Disney World theme park. The attraction was the infamous Astuter Computer Revue that premiered with the opening of Epcot on October 1, 1982, in the CommuniCore East building.

Along the back wall of Epcot Computer Central was a long ramp which led up to a second-floor terraced theater that overlooked a huge room where the park's computers were housed behind large panes of glass. Guests stood to watch the show. The singing and dancing host for the show, who tried to explain the function of these computers in running Epcot, was performer Ken Jennings who was performing as "Earlie the Pearlie," a Cockney pearly busker from the United Kingdom pavilion.

At the Epcot show, guests were shown Jennings performing in the Rose and Crown Pub in the United Kingdom Pavilion and then being electronically transported into the computer room where he was shrunk down to roughly a foot high. He was able to strut across the top of the computers without interrupting the cast members working in the location.

Actually, this was done through an effect known as "Pepper's Ghost" where his image looked like he was in the computer room.

Imagineer George McGinnis explained to Disney enthusiast Lou Mongello:

> We used the same effect (as in the Haunted Mansion), and it was very effective for the little dancing person on the computers. But Tom Fitzgerald secured the people for the parts and all. I laid out the area underneath the guests where the monitors and all the special effects were moving around, unseen by the guests.

During the course of the show (and its successor Backstage Magic), an Audio-Animatronics figure of Mr. Eggz from the Kitchen Kabaret was used (with the same Pepper's Ghost effect) to demonstrate how Audio-Animatronics figures were programmed and operated. At the end of the show, Jennings was returned to full size and transported back to the United Kingdom pavilion.

The Sherman Brothers were called back to the Disney Company by Imagineer Marty Sklar to write a song to explain about being a "rooter for the computer" that many guests have forgotten. Astuter Computer Revue was the first attraction to officially close at Epcot in 1984 and was replaced a month later by a similar but less musical show entitled Backstage Magic.

That show had a perky female hostess named "Julie" (who through the magic of the Pepper's Ghost effect was also shrunk to a foot high and walked on top of the computers) and her little electronic companion I/O (Input/Output). That version closed in October 1993.

Since then, the Epcot computer operation has become much smaller and decentralized and as people joke, the function of all those big mainframes when Epcot opened could probably today be handled on a laptop.

Epcot Fountain
(1982 -2019)

The Fountain of Nations? The Fountain of World Friendship? The CommuniCore Fountain? Innoventions Fountain? Epcot Fountain?

Over the years, the fountain in the middle of Epcot has been called many different names including these titles on official Walt Disney Company press releases. Most guests just referred to it as the Epcot Fountain.

The 180 x 120 foot oval was often used as a central meeting place landmark as well as a photo location with SpaceShip Earth majestically looming in the background.

The iconic fountain has been a part of Epcot since opening day in October 1982. In fact, as a symbolic gesture of international cooperation and understanding, representatives from 22 countries each poured a gallon of water from their homelands into the fountain during the dedication ceremony of the park.

Since 1993 when it was refurbished, the fountain showcased water ballets every fifteen minutes where 304 nozzles and "shooters" propelled water over 150 feet in the air.

There were seven different musical selections that rotated:

- Instrumental from the "Air Battle" sequence from "Surprise in the Skies" a former daytime lagoon show at Epcot
- *"Day One"* by John Tesh
- Main title selection from the Disney live-action feature film *Iron Will*
- *"Mickey's Finale"* selection from a proposed Epcot show tentatively titled "Around the World with Mickey Mouse"
- Selection from Disney's animated feature *The Rescuers Down Under*
- Selection from the Disney live-action feature film *The Rocketeer*
- *"Standing in Motion"* by Yanni

It took three months of computer programming to design the seven different water ballets. At night, 1,068 colored lights highlighted the streams of water. It was the largest fountain on Disney property.

The fountain held approximately one hundred and fifty thousand gallons of water with computer controlled pumps sending almost thirty thousand gallons of water per minute cascading down its tiered walls.

The fountain used almost thirty-five miles of electrical wire. Chloride is too corrosive for this fountain, so Disney used bromine to keep it clean and to ensure that no algae developed. The coins that were retrieved from this fountain, like others on property, were donated by the Disney Company to local charities.

Running underneath the entire fountain was an underground work area that housed the pumps and computer systems, as well as a workshop for cast members who maintained the Epcot fountains. There was also a space with special lifts that were used beneath the stage area for performers and equipment.

The underground work area was built, and then the fountain placed on top, with no planning on how to get new equipment down into the area. Over the years, the fountain had been damaged, like when a temporary stage for performing elephants was put on top of it when Epcot showcased a daily circus.

In the 1980's the fountain team at Walt Disney World included a young civil engineer whose thesis was on the behavior of turbulence-free water. That young engineer, Mark Fuller, worked on the Epcot fountain, and later founded WET Design. This company became the premiere fountain company in the world.

Mark Fuller is also responsible for other Disney fountains including the leapfrog fountain at the Imagination pavilion. His greatest creation to date may be at the Bellagio Hotel in Las Vegas.

The Music of Epcot Center
(1971)

Songwriter Robert Sherman once said, "Walt Disney understood that a song is what people carry away with them. People can go to a Disney picture or park and be enchanted by it, but when they go home, the song is what they keep."

Many of the Sherman Brothers' memorable tunes were composed for Disney animated and live action films. However, they also made significant contributions to the music of the theme parks from *The Tiki, Tiki, Tiki Room* to *It's a Small World* to *There's a Great Big Beautiful Tomorrow*.

Imagineer Marty Sklar told me in an interview in 2007:

> When we were working on Epcot Center, it dawned on us that there hadn't been a new song written for the parks since 1969, not since X Atencio wrote "Grim Grinning Ghosts" for the Haunted Mansion and "Yo Ho, Yo Ho" for the Pirates of the Caribbean. (Atencio along with Buddy Baker would write "It's Fun to Be Free" for the World of Motion pavilion.)

> Thirteen years and no new songs and that needed to be rectified. So we immediately called the Shermans [Richard and Robert Sherman] and told them to start writing songs for Epcot!

One of their first contributions was a theme song for the new park entitled *The World Showcase March* with the opening line: "Oh There's No Place Like World Showcase On The Face Of The Whole Wide World" that premiered as part of the opening ceremonies. They also supplied the songs *One Little Spark* for the Journey Into Imagination pavilion that explained the creation of Figment.

Their song *Magic Journeys* accompanied the 3-D film in the Magic Eye Theater as well they provided the song *Makin' Memories* for the pre-show.

Richard Sherman said:

Kodak's business is all about taking pictures and taking pictures is all about making memories. And with that thought in place, our song was on its way. *Makin' Memories* accompanied a slide show featuring images that ranged from the earliest black and white snapshots to the latest innovations in color photography. Basically, our song was a subliminal commercial pitch for Kodak—no doubt the 'softest sell' in the history of singing commercials!

They also provided the *Computer Song* for the Astuter Computer Revue sung by Ken Jennings who was also performing in the United Kingdom pavilion.

Sklar told me:

They wrote some great stuff but with so many pavilions, they couldn't write everything. We brought in a young California songwriter named Bob Moline and took a chance. He had made an impression when he had performed for a group of Disneyland executives during a private function.

We had him write a jingle for Disneyland, *It Could Only Happen at Disneyland*, and the advertisement won a CLIO Award. He was performing at a bar in Newport Beach.

His contribution to the sound of Epcot is often forgotten. He wrote or co-wrote songs like *Listen to the Land* for the Land pavilion, *Canada You're a Lifetime Journey* for the Canada pavilion, *Golden Dream* for the American pavilion with Randy Bright and, of course, *Energy You Make the World Go 'Round* for the Universe of Energy that played during the pre-show and was sung by John Joyce. Academy Award winning songwriters Al Kasha and Joel Hirschhorn wrote the theme song *Universe of Energy* that was at the end of the attraction.

Moline died on December 11, 2011. Later in life, he worked primarily in religious music and it was rumored he had written a musical about Walt and his brother Roy that was never produced.

Ice Station Cool/ Club Cool

(1998 – 2019)

Disney has had a long relationship with Coca-Cola since it was one of the original lessees at Disneyland in 1955 and became the sole soft drink provider for the Disney theme parks in 1982 when it started sponsoring the American Adventure pavilion at Epcot.

Club Cool sold Coca-Cola souvenirs as well as offering guests unlimited free samples of different variations of the classic beverage from around the world, very much like a much smaller version of the World of Coca-Cola location in Coke's corporate headquarters of Atlanta, Georgia. "Learn how the world refreshes itself!"

- Italy – Beverly — A bitter flavor but is a popular non-alcoholic aperitif.
- Greece – Fanta Pineapple — One of ninety different Fanta flavors, this caffeine-free offering has a sweet pineapple taste.
- Thailand – Fanta Melon Frosty
- Japan – Vegitabeta — A non-carbonated apricot and passion fruit mix
- South Africa – Bilbo — Fruit flavored lime juice
- Zimbabwe – Sparletta – Raspberry flavored cream soda
- Peru – Inca Kola — A sweet fruity flavor some say is similar to bubblegum.
- Brazil – Gurana Kuat — Guarana berry flavored

Originally the location opened as Ice Station Cool in June 1998 with a themed entrance near the Innoventions Fountain. It closed on June 6, 2005 and was reformatted into Club Cool that opened in November.

Welcome to Ice Station Cool, the most refreshing place on Earth. Coca-Cola "Coolologists" have been searching the globe non-stop for years, hoping to discover the origin of cool. This place is a recreation of one of the Coolologist's recent Refreshus Maximus (Maximum Refreshment) expeditions.

The name of the location had been inspired by the 1963 Alistair MacLean novel *Ice Station Zebra* about a British meterological station built on an ice floe in the Arctic Sea that was made into a popular 1968 movie. The idea came from the actual Ice Station Alpha and Ice Station Bravo that were established in the Arctic during The International Geophysical Year 1957-1958.

Another inspiration for the theming was the "The Iceman", a 5,300 year old corpse discovered September 19, 1991 on the border of Italy and Austria (in the Alps) who had been buried in ice since the Neolithic Era and was completely preserved including items like his dagger and a copper axe.

"The story (of Ice Station Cool) is a group of archeologists made this discovery high in the sub-arctic," said principal production designer Kerry Gilman. "But El Nino caused the ice to melt, so Refreshus Maximus (the name given by the expedition to the frozen Neanderthal) found reaching for a bottle of The Real Thing was brought to be preserved and studied at Epcot, the land of discovery."

Guests entered a snow cave opening just past a snow cat and exterior misters exuding a fine, cold spray. Going through sliding doors and hanging freezer flaps, they find themselves in an insulated concrete tunnel featuring the remains (behind glass) of a recently discovered frozen Neanderthal from "a 30,000 year old highly civilized and now highly frozen refreshment culture" in a faux ice wall.

Throughout the 85 foot long cave, a snow machine pumped four tons of shaved ice per twelve hour period. That equals 240 cubic feet, roughly the equivalent of a ten by twenty foot room covered in a foot of flurries and had to be cleared out every night. A two inch trough was placed below special floor grates to catch any melting flakes so that the area did not become flooded.

Universe of Energy/ Ellen's Energy Adventure

(1982 – 2017)

From its opening in October 1982 until its renovation in September 1996, the pavilion told a fairly serious and educational story about energy and the energy needs of the future.

Disney had to go through forty different scripts because the sponsor Exxon wanted to focus more on fossil fuels with other alternative sources like nuclear, solar and wind power being relegated to still experimental possibilities unable to meet current energy needs. However, there was an independent board known as The Epcot Center Energy Advisory Committee who also had to approve so a compromise was finally made.

From its re-design in 1996 until its closing in 2017, the pavilion shared a more light-hearted story about energy centered on comedian Ellen DeGeneres' learning about the topic in a nightmare. The official grand opening was on October 1, 1996.

Show director Robert Ginty said:

> People can go anyplace and just see a movie. What we've done here is create what is truly a one-of-a kind theme park experience that will not only entertain people but give them the feeling they've learned something as well. I think the way that most people want to learn is to be entertained. You want to pay attention if it's fun.

Ellen falls asleep on her couch while watching the popular television game show *Jeopardy*. She dreams she is a contestant on the show and is pitted against her nemesis from college, Dr. Judy Peterson (actress Jamie Lee Curtis) and Dr. Albert Einstein. All the categories in Ellen's nightmare game show deal with energy so, by the halfway point in the game, she is losing terribly. She calls upon her next door neighbor Bill Nye the Science Guy to give her (and the guests in the vehicle) a crash course about energy.

The birth of the universe—in one minute—across three, 70mm screens, 157-feet wide by 32-feet tall was shown. Next, the theater separated into six, 97-passenger vehicles that traveled through the primeval dioramas.

Each vehicle was driven by a single six horsepower electric motor powered by eight 12-volt lead-acid automotive batteries. These batteries recharged during the show while the theater cars were in their stationary formation on the huge turntables.

The cars were guided by a wire, 1/8-inch thick that was embedded in the concrete floor and emitted a low level radio frequency. The vehicle was in constant communication with a computer that issued the speed, start, stop, and turn commands for the vehicle through the wire.

After the dioramas, guests entered into another theater, where they viewed a dramatic motion picture on three screens, each 30-feet tall by 74-feet wide that curved to create a 200-degree range of vision. In Nye's Science Helicopter, Ellen learned about the world's present-day energy needs, resources, and concerns. She learns that brain power is the one energy source that will never run out.

The show closed in 2017 to make way for a new attraction themed to the Marvel movie franchise Guardians of the Galaxy.

One of the longest attractions in terms of time expenditure (the pre-show in the lobby ran roughly eight minutes followed by 37 minutes trapped in slow-moving vehicles), fewer and fewer guests were willing to invest that amount of their day, even though the air-conditioning provided a welcome break from the Orlando heat and humidity, and waits in lines for other attractions were just as long or longer.

Universe of Energy Photovoltaic Cells

(1982 -2017)

According to a Disney press release from October 1982:

> The Universe of Energy experience begins with our first glimpse of the building's exterior. Its dynamic shape is itself an expression of energy. A wedge-shaped structure with the apex of its enormous triangle tilted toward the ground, it appears to be simultaneously rising out of the earth and driving into it.
>
> Warm bands of color, symbolic of radiating heat, alternate along its sides. As we approach we notice that this slanting roof glistens with a blanket of solar panels.
>
> The mammoth array of photovoltaic cells faces the sun, drawing in its energy and converting it into electrical current. This combination of the functional and the aesthetic is a subliminal statement of the pavilion's overall theme; that by exploring and developing alternative energy sources we can build an energy-bridge to a better tomorrow.
>
> As we near the apex, we notice a separate structure standing in front of the main building. Its mirrored surface reflects the images of rippling water from a pool below – the reflections seem to suggest energy in motion. Beyond the reflecting pool is the main entrance.

One of the original concepts for the pavilion was having nearby a solar dish and a parabolic shaped mirror that would concentrate sunlight into a superheated receptacle and then transfer that energy to the actual building.

Since a major part of the story was that photovoltaic cells on the roof, in the form of 2,156 solar panels, would help power the pavilion, in particular the theater vehicles, careful study was done in terms of the shape of the building, as well as its location in the park to best collect sunlight.

At best, perhaps fifteen percent of the power for the pavilion came from the cels but Disney publicity proclaimed that guests were "riding on sunshine".

Imagineers tracked the sun as it moved over the property and determined that the 105,000 square foot structure should be anchored facing southward and tilted 30 degrees from the horizon. Starting at roughly 20 feet above the entrance to the pavilion, the roof slopes upward to a height of nearly 60 feet at the rear.

Across its width sat the array of photovoltaic cells and, at the time of its construction, it was the largest privately funded solar power installation in the world.

Each of the four-inch round silicon solar cells captured photon energy from sunlight and converted it to approximately one watt of electrical energy. Thirty-six individual cells were wired in series and housed in an aluminum framed module.

Almost 2,200 modules made up the photovoltaic array and together generated approximately 70,000 watts of direct current power. The power was fed through an inverter that converted it to alternating current, to the utility power grid and supplied enough power nearly equal to that used in the ride system.

The original exterior was painted in transitioning sections of deep red to orange to yellow, suggesting radiating energy. With the changes in 1996, the red to yellow motif was repainted a deep blue with rainbow pastel highlights.

Dinosaur topiaries were shipped to Epcot from New York's Rockefeller Center where they were once part of a Flower & Garden Festival and installed outside the entrance in 1996. The Brontosaurus topiary kept suffering damage from guests hanging from its neck and all the topiaries were removed in 2009.

When Exxon Mobil did not renew their sponsorship in 2004, all references to the company were removed. In 2009, the pavilion's basic original color scheme of yellow was restored.

Universe of Energy Dinosaurs
(1982 2017)

While it is now agreed that over ninety percent of oil came from a bio-mass of prehistoric trees and vegetation, generations of people grew up thinking that the oil and gas coming out of the ground was from decomposed dinosaurs, a concept that many people still believe today.

In the "Rite of Spring" sequence in the animated feature *Fantasia* (1940), Walt Disney and his talented artists brought back to life extinct creatures that garnered accolades in the scientific community. The sequence included Pterodactyls on rock outcroppings while a herd of Brontosauruses quietly grazed in a lake.

One of the most memorable scenes was a climactic battle between a Stegosaurus and a vicious Tyrannosaurus Rex that could never have happened, since those animals lived in different eras, but it was highly memorable and dramatic. Walt recreated those exact same images in three-dimensions for the 1964-65 New York World's Fair Ford Motor Skyway attraction.

After the fair was over, that primeval world scene with forty-six audio-animatronics dinosaurs was relocated to the finale of the Grand Canyon Diorama on the Santa Fe & Disneyland railroad in July 1966 and remains there today.

The Universe of Energy pavilion at Epcot offers a seven minute journey through a scenic backdrop diorama surrounding a primeval forest. The diorama stretches 32 feet high, 515 feet across and took three artists nearly 6,000 hours to paint.

Of course, no pictures exist of such a location so the Imagineers consulted well known paleontologists and paleo-botanists to learn as much as they could about the plants and animals of millions of years ago.

Hundreds of books, publications, museum plates and exhibits and fossils were reviewed. Imagineers even used research to try to approximate the actual sounds prehistoric creatures might have made.

However, this was not meant to be a museum but an entertainment so certain things were exaggerated and sometimes recreated bigger than they probably were for dramatic effect.

The thirty-six dinosaurs were the largest audio-animatronics animals ever to be fabricated by Imagineering. They were so huge that they had to be placed in the building first and then the roof installed overhead.

The forest is landscaped with 250 pre-historic trees that rise up to 40 feet overhead. A lightweight foamed plastic, similar to the cellulose structure of the plants' woody pulp was used to capture the tensile and compressive characteristics of a real tree that would "sway with the breeze". The plastics used to fabricate the trees were actually made from the fossil fuels created by the real trees of pre-history.

Fog fills the warm show room, along with swampy smells made by WED Smellitzers. The biggest dinosaurs in the swamp are giant brontosauruses eating water plants. Duck-billed trachodons are seen bathing in a pool of water. A number of Ornithomimus watch helpless as one of their own sinks into a boiling tar pit. Numerous Pteranodons perch menacingly on cliffs and rocks.

And, of course on an overhead cliff a Stegosaurus fights another dinosaur that was reconfigured to be the more historically accurate Allosaurus.

On September 15, 1996, after a rehab, Universe of Energy reopened with the subtitle "Ellen's Energy Adventure." For a short time, the subtitle was "Ellen's Energy Crisis," but then changed to "Adventure."

Because of the latest research that indicated that dinosaurs were more like birds than lizards, the audio-animatronics creatures were repainted brighter with more stripes and markings. The flora was rehabbed as well.

Body Wars
(1989 - 2017)

Both Star Tours and Body Wars attractions use a simulator (Rediffusion ATLAS-Advanced Technology Leisure Application Simulator) that consists of a cabin supported by six servo actuators ("legs").

The actuators are powered hydraulically and driven automatically using electrical drive signals received from a free-standing motion-control cabinet.

The actuators provide "six degree of freedom movement" so the cabin can be moved in planes representing heave, surge and sway and in axes representing pitch, roll and yaw independently or in any combination.

In fact, the success of Star Tours in 1987 inspired the Imagineers to try developing an "inner space" attraction of a miniaturized submarine-like probe journeying through a patient's body just like in the film *Fantastic Voyage (1966)* for the "Wonders of Life" pavilion at Epcot in 1989.

The new attraction was called *Body Wars* most likely because WDW guests called *Star Tours* the *Star Wars* ride or just *Star Wars*.

The probe's captain, Jack Braddock (Tim Matheson from *Animal House*) sets out on a fairly routine medical mission with a crew of civilian observers accompanying him. The submarine and crew were miniaturized by a "particle reducer" to the size of a single cell and beamed inside the human body to rendezvous with Dr. Cynthia Lair (Elizabeth Shue who starred in Disney's *Adventures in Babysitting*), an immunologist who also has been miniaturized to study the body's response to a splinter lodged beneath the skin.

Unfortunately, the mission becomes a high-speed race against time when Dr. Lair is swept from the splinter site into the rush of the bloodstream.

Through the pounding chambers of the patient's heart and through the lungs' gale-force winds, the ship rode the body's current in an effort to rescue Dr. Lair. Even after she was safely on board, there are still problems when the ship loses power and heads toward the brain in search of emergency power and escape.

The film was directed by Leonard "Mr. Spock" Nimoy who had recently finished directing Touchstone's *Three Men and a Baby (1987)*. With anatomical images produced by computer graphics and special effects film techniques, it was a remarkably realistic experience.

"Even though Body Wars is the shortest film I've ever directed, it presented a new set of challenges," said Nimoy at the time. "We had to take into account that the film will be shown inside a moving theater -- the simulator. So, in order to intensify the sense of motion, we built a set that actually moves, and rocked it during filming to match the pitching and rolling of the simulator."

When the ride was being programmed, an Imagineer watched the film repeatedly while moving a computer joystick to indicate movement and to synchronize the ride and the film.

Since the story of the attraction was that guests were in the bloodstream, the Imagineers programmed in movement to mimic the beat of a pulse. That additional movement may be the movement that unsettled countless guests who had survived a similar experience on *Star Tours* without any ill effects.

Some Walt Disney Imagineers felt that it was just the images of being inside a human body with all the yucky "blood and guts" that generated feelings of unease.

The attraction officially closed when the Wonders of Life pavilion closed on January 1, 2007. The simulators were eventually stripped for parts for the Star Tours attraction at Disney's Hollywood Studios, so it would be very difficult for Body Wars to once again be brought back to life and rush through the circulatory and respiratory systems and make guests queasy.

Cranium Command
(1989 - 2007)

Cranium Command opened at Epcot October 19, 1989 as part of the new Wonders of Life pavilion, sponsored by Metropolitan Life Insurance Company (MetLife). The premise of the attraction directed by Jerry Rees is that the guest is inside the head of a twelve year old boy (voiced by Scott Curtis) who is being piloted by a new, young, inexperienced recruit named Buzzy.

Guests meet Buzzy as an animated character and learn his mission and the consequences for failure in the pre-show directed by Kirk Wise and Gary Trousdale. It was the very last project at Disney Feature Animation to be traditionally inked and painted on cels. Pete Docter was an animator on the project and later admitted that it helped inspire his own Pixar feature film *Inside Out*.

The direction of the five minute pre- show animation segment was so impressive that Disney executive Jeffrey Katzenberg assigned Wise and Trousdale to direct the animated feature *Beauty and the Beast* and later *Hunchback of Notre Dame*.

Wise, by the way, provides the monotone voice for the Hypothalamus after the guests entered the main 200 seat auditorium where Buzzy was now portrayed by an audio-animatronics figure.

On several screens, celebrity actors including Charles Grodin, Jon Lovitz, Kevin Nealon, Dana Carvey, Bobcat Goldthwait, Kevin Meaney and George Wendt play various body functions like the left and right brain, the ventricles of the heart, adrenal gland and stomach. Their humorous responses to the various activities help explain the function of those organs.

In a seventeen minute show, Buzzy had to deal with a typical day of misadventures at school from missing the school bus to an accident in chemistry class to dealing with bullies and an infatuation with a female schoolmate. It was the hope that the show might be reprogrammed over the years to tell different stories dealing with how the body functions rather than just stress management.

MetLife ended its sponsorship of the Wonders of Life by June 2001. Although the MetLife logos disappeared from the pavilion, Cranium Command and most of the pavilion's other attractions continued to operate normally through 2003. In 2004, the Wonders of Life pavilion became seasonal and was open fewer days each year.

On New Year's Day 2007, the Wonders of Life was officially closed. The domed pavilion became the Festival Center for Epcot's Food & Wine Festival in fall and for Epcot's Flower & Garden Festival in spring.

In February 2018, Disney announced that it would become the *PLAY!* Pavilion, "a digital metropolis where guests will discover an interactive city bursting with games, activities and experiences that connect them with friends, family and beloved Disney characters—both real and virtual—like never before."

A still unsolved mystery is what happened to the Buzzy audio-animatronics figure that disappeared from the closed attraction. The pressurized hydraulic lines were clumsily cut in order to remove the heavy figure.

According to the Orlando police report Patrick Allen Spikes was charged with the theft and selling of Buzzy's jacket, headset and hat that ended up in the possession of NBA player Robin Lopez. However Spikes denied taking the figure itself which is still missing, despite some reports that a Disney department removed it without informing any other departments.

The Making of Me
(1989 - 2007)

The Making of Me was a fourteen minute film attraction written and directed by Glenn Gordon Caron, creator of television's *Moonlighting* series, starring actor Martin Short that opened in the Wonders of Life pavilion in October 1989.

In the early 1980s, Disney proposed a "Life and Health" pavilion for Epcot that would be sponsored by Humana Inc., the hospital-management and health-insurance company. Humana wanted to stress medical technology instead of health.

John Creedon, then chief executive officer and president of Metropolitan Life Insurance Co. of New York, was more interested in a health-related project and agreed to sponsor the pavilion. Creedon came up with the "Wonders of Life" name for the pavilion and also named the "Body Wars" attraction.

Under terms of its sponsorship, MetLife agreed not to use any of the Peanuts characters it had used in its advertising since 1985 in the 100,000 square foot, ninety million dollar pavilion.

Imagineer Barry Braverman said, "The goal was to produce an informative, tasteful piece with a Disney touch. It's a cross between the technology of the science series, *Nova*, and the time-travel theme of the movie, *Back to The Future* (1985) where Short discovers how his parents gave birth to him. It's a way for the viewer to reconnect with the experience of being born."

The animated portion showed a sperm fertilizing an egg, but there is no mention of how the sperm got there leaving it up to parents to explain that aspect. The scene is the "Uterus City Limits" on the day of the big race. The star: a fertile egg cell who wears a blond ponytail and red lipstick. Her supporting cast: thousands of blue Pac-Man-style sperm cells.

As the tension mounts, one speedy sperm collides with the egg in a theatrical explosion of light, fog and mist. A new baby has been conceived. Some children were confused by the animation whether real babies were made that way.

The film, prefaced by a warning to parents, includes footage of a live human birth and photography taken inside the womb. The entire movie was done in just four months and finished at "virtually the last possible instant" said Braverman.

Eisner did not care for earlier concepts because they didn't blend dramatic footage by Swedish cinematographer Lennart Nilson with the human context. The photographs of fetal development had appeared in the PBS *Nova* series episode *Miracle of Life*.

It was Eisner who brought in Caron and only asked for one change.

"He said, 'Glenn, do you really think the parents should meet in high school? We don't want people thinking we think they should have children right out of high school'," Caron recalled.

Caron agreed to the change. Short's parents now meet at a college dance.

Dr. Robert John Haggerty, a member of the Wonders of Life Advisory Board stated when the pavilion opened, "This film can be a good conversation starter. A fair number of parents need this kind of basic information to get over their own anxieties about sex education."

Lawrence W. Green, a California public health specialist who was also a member of the advisory board, agreed that once parents "get over the shock of seeing the reproductive process revealed so frankly," they will see the benefits of the film. "There is a long history of attempts to simplify this information. Many parents underestimate the degree that kids are getting this information independent of legitimate sources."

World of Motion

(1982 -1996)

The World of Motion sponsored by General Motors was an opening day attraction in Future World and continued to operate until January 1996. It was eventually replaced by Test Track that was also sponsored by GM.

GM had signed a commitment to a transportation pavilion in 1977 making it the first official Epcot pavilion participant.

The dark ride omnimover vehicle attraction was designed by Imagineer Mark David with significant contribution from Disney Legends Marc Davis and later Ward Kimball in staging the various tableaus.

It was a whimsical look at the history of transportation from caveman's "foot power" to the first traffic jam (of a motor car smashing into a horse-drawn produce cart) to modern day with thirty-one amusing scenes featuring approximately 140 comically exaggerated audio-animatronics figures as well as projection effects.

The exterior of the pavilion showed the blue omnimover vehicles slowly spiraling clockwise from the ground floor up to the second level before entering a contoured hole in the red wall.

The narrator of the attraction was radio personality Gary Owens who told guests:

> General Motors now invites you to travel the open road - to discover that when it comes to transportation, it's always fun to be free! Throughout the ages, we have searched for freedom to move from one place to another.

The theme song, *It's Fun To Be Free*, composed by Buddy Baker with lyrics by Xavier "X" Atencio was repeated during the experience in a variety of styles from ragtime, Dixieland jazz, Broadway show tune, symphonic, Copland-esque western, kazoo and more. The two song writers had previously collaborated on *Grim Grinning Ghosts* for the Haunted Mansion.

The journey on the 1,730 feet of track ended after a trip through a "speed tunnel" at the sixty foot high CenterCore, a city of tommorow in perpetual motion that included a Pepper's Ghost illusion to put guests into futuristic bubble cars.

The narration intoned:

> Yes, our world has indeed become a world of motion. We have engineered marvels that take us swiftly over land and sea, through the air and into space itself. And still bolder and better ideas are yet to come, ideas that will fulfill our age-old dream to be free; free in mind, free in spirit, free to follow the distant star of our ancestors to a brighter tomorrow.

Guests then disembarked into the Transcenter designed by Bob Rogers and his BRC Imagination Arts studio that featured several hands-on experiences that showcased what the engineers at GM were developing for future transportation.

A GM promotional brochure stated:

> The Trancenter showcases candid, behind the scenes views of what it takes to design, engineer, and manufacture cars and trucks with the highest order of quality and imagination.
>
> But satisfying today's personal travel requirements is only part of the ongoing creative process. Anticipating what lies ahead is another story that comes to life in the GM Transcenter. Clearly, The Future of Transportation is Here...and on full display!

Guests could design a car through computer modeling, view an animated film about different types of engines, visit a display of options for the interior of a future car, or be entertained by The Bird and the Robot show where an audio-animatronics toucan interacted with "Tiger" an assembly-line robot arm.

While the attraction attracted approximately 20,000 guests a day who enjoyed the experience, GM wanted something more of a thrill attraction that focused solely on automobiles which resulted in the development of Test Track in the same location.

Horizons
(1983 – 1999)

Horizons was an omnimover dark ride in Future World that focused on how families would live in the 21st Century on desert farms, in outer space, and under the sea and how advances in technology would make all that possible.

It opened in October 1983, temporarily closed in 1994 after General Electric dropped its sponsorship of the attraction, briefly reopened periodically and permanently closed in January 1999. It was replaced by Mission: SPACE.

Mission: SPACE includes tributes to the Horizons attraction that preceeded it including the center of the gravity wheel in the queue having the attraction logo, and a stylized version of the logo appearing on the front of the checkout counter in the Cargo Bay gift shop at the exit to the attraction.

The official description for Horizons was "dedicated to humanity's future. It is a careful synthesis of all the wonders within Epcot, and applies the elements of communication, energy, transportation, creativity, and technology to a better life-style for the family of the future."

The attraction was generally considered a spiritual sequel to the Carousel of Progress attraction previously sponsored by GE. Horizons featured all the key elements associated with the original Epcot: communication, community interaction, energy, transportation, anatomy, physiology, imagination along with man's relationship to the sea, land, air, and space.

The attraction was developed by Imagineer George McGinnis who at one point considered calling it New Horizons. That phrase became the name of the attraction's theme song written by George Wilkins. The message of the pavilion that "If you can dream it, then you can do it" is often falsely attributed to Walt Disney.

Imagineering Show Writer Tom Fitzgerald said:

> I am very familiar with that line because I wrote it! It was written specifically for the *Horizons* attraction at Epcot and used in numerous ways, from dialogue in the ride to graphics.

In fact, Fitzgerald appeared in the attraction. "Tom II," the submarine-repairing boyfriend, was an audio-animatronic that looked just like Fitzgerald and he provided the voice. Fitzgerald was later given the figure when the attraction was demolished.

At the exit of the attraction was a large wall painting done by famed space artist Bob McCall entitled "The Prologue and the Promise". It was a gorgeous image of a family standing on a mountaintop facing a bright future with famous monuments of the past and future. It was later covered up and replaced.

The attraction began with a look back at how the future was perceived and transitioned into modern technologies that might be used in the world of tomorrow. The main portion of the ride focused on life in the future in different habitats.

The end of the ride allowed guests to select one of three different routes to return to FuturePort: from the space station Brava Centauri, the desert farm of Mesa Verde or the Sea Castle research base.

These thirty-one second video sequences featured a video fly-through of elaborate scale models. The model for the desert route was 32 by 75 feet long. All the models were filmed at a hangar at the Burbank airport. It took a year to build and shoot the three segments.

Orange Fragrance Scent R-2534 dispersed by air cannon during the attraction was produced by Felton International Inc. in Los Angeles, California and is still available. Many of the props from the attraction were sent to Tokyo DisneySea and Disneyland Paris (Solo Sub and hovercraft) as well as being auctioned off to private collectors.

Journey Into Imagination
(1982 – 1998)

Journey Into Imagination did not officially open until March 5, 1983 and closed in 1998. Dreamfinder and Figment were considered the official spokes-characters for Epcot and appeared prominently in the attraction. A walk-around costumed Dreamfinder manipulating a Figment puppet delighted guests at the park for roughly fifteen years.

In ride vehicles, the guests found themselves floating among the clouds where they encountered Dreamfinder piloting his Dream Catcher blimp collecting dreams and ideas in its bag which is how he created Figment.

The guests then journeyed to the Dreamport filled with everything Dreamfinder had collected. Next they would journey through the Realms of Imagination represented in rooms dedicated to Art, Literature, the Performing Arts and Science.

The final room had Figment standing on a giant film canister surrounded by movie screens of him in various roles including scientist, mountain climber, pirate, cowboy, superhero, athlete and more.

Guests were then encouraged to explore their imagination in the Image Works, an interactive exhibit described as a creative playground on the upper floor.

The little purple dragon, Figment, was the physical representation of "a figment of the Imagination." The Sherman Brothers theme song for the attraction, *One Little Spark*, described the character as "Two tiny wings, eyes big and yellow, horns of a steer, but a lovable fellow. From head to tail, he's royal purple pigment, and there, voila, you've got a Figment."

Dreamfinder was his husky human companion and friend with a full red beard, long blue coat, black top hat and broad smile supposedly modeled after the physical appearance of Imagineer Joe Rohde.

Figment and Dreamfinder were from a concept for a planned-but-never-built section of Disneyland to be called Discovery Bay where guests would visit Professor Marvel's Gallery of Illusion, including Marvel's collection of dragons.

Imagineer Tony Baxter used a small concept statue of Marvel cradling a small green dragon to convince potential sponsor Kodak to invest in the pavilion devoted to imagination hosted by a character originally called Dreamkeeper.

Imagineer Steve Kirk remembered:

> They said, "That's great, do we get the dragon, too?"' The only issue was that, at the time, the dragon was painted green. And Kodak thought that represented a little too much of a Fuji Film (Kodak's chief competitor who used the color green prominently on its packaging) connection, so he turned purple as a result of that.

Tony Baxter recalled:

> [Dreamfinder] was a Santa Claus-type who is wise and older and knows all the great things, a great thinker. But we needed a childlike character that had like a one second attention span and was a little crazy.

To provide the voice for Dreamfinder, WED hired actor Chuck McCann who based the voice on actor Frank Morgan as the mighty Wizard in MGM's *The Wizard of Oz* (1939). Actor Billy Barty did the voice for Figment.

Actor Ron Schneider first appeared as a live action Dreamfinder with a Figment puppet on opening day where he was interviewed by Bryan Gumbel on the NBC *Today* show. Later, Steve Taylor became Schneider's understudy and then took over the role full time for almost fifteen years when Schneider went on to other projects.

Taylor was significantly shorter than Schneider so it was just assumed that like Figment, the character could be any size he wanted.

The attraction was later replaced by Journey Into YOUR Imagination featuring Figment and Dr. Nigel Channing the chairman of the Imagination Institute in 1999.

Kitchen Kabaret
(1982 - 1994)

Kitchen Kabaret was a thirteen minute audio-animatronics show in The Land pavilion that opened in 1982. The audio-animatronics show promoted good nutrition through songs and comedy featuring anthropomorphic vaudeville-styled food characters who appeared in the kitchen of hostess Bonnie Appetite.

The show promoted healthy eating and the importance of the four food groups: meat, dairy, grains and fruits/vegetables.

Kraft Central Foods sponsored the entire pavilion at the time. Show writer Randy Bright said, "Kitchen Kabaret with performing foodstuffs will be like the bear band at Magic Kingdom."

The prologue to the show was a blonde-haired, pretty Bonnie Appetite attired as a housewife in her kitchen with her oversized cookbooks and singing *Meal Time Blues* about the drudgery of preparing another meal.

In the first act, Bonnie in a glittery cocktail waitress costume sings *Chase Those Meal Time Blues Away* with the Kitchen Krackpots (condiments in Kraft packaging including ketchup, mayonnaise, and mustard).

The second act focused on characters from the refrigerator surrounded by dry ice fog featuring a singing milk carton named Mr. Dairy Goods and three dairy products: Miss Cheese, Miss Yogurt and Miss Ice Cream who all proclaimed their benefits. Act three had The Cereal Sisters (Rennie Rice, Connie Corn and Mairzy Oats) singing *Boogie Woogie Bakery Boy* accompanied by a bugle blowing slice of bread who they sang was "the toast of the town".

Act four had the comedy team of Hamm and Eggz sharing wisecracks in a derisive manner to each other and singing about meat as good protein accompanied by animated slides.

Act five featured the Colander Combo and the Fiesta Fruit (with Bonnie in a Carmen Miranda style outfit perched on a crescent moon) singing the memorable *Veggie Veggie Fruit Fruit* song.

The broccoli who kept saying "cha-cha-cha" in this scene was supposedly inspired by the hair style and glasses of Imagineer Barry Braverman. Blaine Gibson sculpted the maquette for the broccoli figure.

> There are no substitutes for we.
> Veggie fruit fruit. Veggie veggie fruit fruit.
> You see (can't you see) a balanced meal always wins with our vitamins, A and C.
> Si si fruit fruit.
> Veggie veggie fruit fruit.
> Veggie fruit fruit.

The Kabaret Finale had Bonnie and the entire cast singing a medley of songs.

At the show's exit was a shop called Broccoli & Co. that offered merchandise of the characters including placemats, magnets, note pads, plush figures, coloring books, audio tapes, postcards and pins. It eventually converted to just selling generic kitchen ware.

Imagineer Eric Jacobsen worked on the model for the attraction and said in 1980, "This model has taken about a year to complete. Most of the show has been decided on before the model is even started. Sometimes better solutions may come up as I'm working. Right now I'm working on colors and props and details."

Nestle took over sponsorship of The Land in 1994. In addition to changing Listen to the Land to Living with the Land, replacing the film *Symbiosis* with *Circle of Life: An Environmental Fable*, the company updated the pavilion's entire dining and shopping area.

Nestle wanted to update Kitchen Kabaret to feature updated music and be more entertaining than educational so the show was replaced with Food Rocks in 1994.

The twelve minute audio-animatronics show was a benefit concert for good nutrition hosted by Fud Wrapper who was continually interrupted by Excess, a junk food heavy metal band. The twelve songs parodied famous tunes. That attraction closed in 2004 to be replaced by Soarin' Over California that opened in 2005.

Maelstrom

(1988 – 2014)

The Norway Pavilion was the 11th and final (so far) country added to Epcot's World Showcase in 1988. Norwegian Showcase (NorShow) was a consortium of eleven companies established to pay for the pavilion and represent Norwegian interests. The Norwegian government also helped pay for the pavilion.

Disney Imagineers proposed an attraction called SeaVenture where guests would ride along a 946-foot water flume encountering trolls and gnomes, and the legends about them with a theme song written by the Sherman Brothers. Another proposal was Vikings on their way on the Rainbow Bridge to Valhalla.

The Norwegian sponsors wanted the attraction to be more of a travelogue to encourage increased tourism. NorShow gave the Imagineers a list of items they wanted shown in the attraction that they felt uniquely related to the story of Norway including Vikings, a fishing village, a polar bear, a fjord and an oil rig and perhaps, if there was room, a troll or two.

Attraction Designer Bob Kurzweil came up with the new approach that it would be a time-travel experience through the history of Norway to give guests the experience that "those who seek the spirit of Norway face peril and adventure, but more often find beauty and charm."

Disney Imagineer Randy Bright stated:

> It's the first ride that actually goes backwards, and the first ride that will utilize Audio-Animatronics in a black light environment.

An Epcot press release at the time described the attraction as "Visitors take a fantasy voyage that departs a modern-day village on a Norwegian fjord and journeys up a cascading waterway into the Norway of old. The trip is aboard small ships patterned after the dragon-headed craft of Eric the Red and his fellow explorers."

The boats were some of the first concept art work done by Imagineer Joe Rohde for Walt Disney World. It was also some of the last work done by famed Imagineer Jack Ferges, who built the model for the ride vehicle ship and also sculpted the polar bear maquettes.

Originally, the polar bear (who stood eleven feet tall) scene was going to feature extensive rockwork but, to cut costs, most of it was replaced with black-light painted flats.

Adding to the attraction's appeal would be various drops including one of twenty-eight feet and visual effects, as well as a unique directional change with the ride vehicle briefly going outside over a waterfall and then back in to the attraction and backward. The new designs also called for a full-scale replication of a North Sea storm to include wind, waves, rain, thunder and real lightning.

Over the years, there were a few minor changes made to the attraction. The smoke effects in both the Troll scene and the reverse scene were toned down. The wave and rain effects in the North Sea Storm scene were also muted, and the Tesla coil that originally created the lightning effect over the oil rig was replaced with strobe lights.

At the end of the boat ride was a theater showing a six-minute film entitled The *Spirit of Norway* directed by Paul Gerber about the beauty of present day Norway. In later years, guests often walked straight through the theater rather than watching the outdated film.

NorShow sold back its interest in the pavilion to Disney in 1992. In September 2014, Disney announced that the attraction would be replaced with a new attraction based on the animated feature *Frozen* (2013) that would immerse guests in favorite moments from the film.

Wonders of China
(1982 – 2002)

When Epcot's China Pavilion opened in 1982, it featured a Circle-Vision 360 degree movie called *Wonders of China: Land of Beauty, Land of Time* that gave foreigners a glimpse of areas of China that had rarely been seen before by outsiders. This film closed in March 2002 and was replaced in May 2003 with a new movie called *Reflections of China*.

The Disney crew was the first Western film group to be allowed to film certain sites. During early negotiations, the Chinese government denied permission to film any locations considered "strategic", such as bridges, tunnels, and trains or filming anywhere near an Army base.

By the end of production, the crew had proven to be cooperative and the footage shot so impressive that the government gave permission for a shot of train coming out of a tunnel and across a river bridge as well as another shot that was made of peasants and water buffaloes on the property of an Army base.

The final nineteen minute presentation featured such landmarks as Beijing's Forbidden City; vast, wide-open Mongolia and its stern-faced tribesmen; the 2,400-year-old Great Wall; the eight centuries old Great Buddha of Leshan; the muddy Yangtze River and the 3,000-year-old city of Suzhou, whose location on the Grand Canal, which is generally believed to be the largest man-made waterway in the world, which encouraged Marco Polo to call it the Venice of the East.

In addition, there were shots of Shanghai, as well as Hangzhou, where a handful of Chinese are shown doing their morning exercises along the river's edge. Also shown are Huangshan Mountain, wreathed in fog; the Shilin Stone Forest of jagged rock outcroppings in Yunnan Province; Urumqi, whose distance from the sea in Xinjiang Province earned it the title of the most inland city on earth; Lahsa, in Tibet, and its Potala Palace, boasting a thousand rooms and ten times that many altars.

Also shown were the Reed Flute Cave and the bizarrely shaped hills of Kweilin above, to say nothing of the very European-looking city of Shanghai. To complete the picture, there are fields of snow and of wheat, high meadows and beaches dotted with tropical palms, harbors and rice terraces, calligraphers, checkers and Ping-Pong players, lightning-fast acrobats, championship horseback riders, camels and a panda bear, glittering ice sculptures, and millions of bicycles.

The Birnbaum guide stated, "Every step of the way, the film crews were besieged by curious Chinese, even in empty Mongolia. For the Huangshan Mountain sequence, which lasts only seconds, the crew and about three dozen hired laborers had to carry the 600-pound camera uphill for nearly a mile. The Chinese government would not permit Disney cameramen to shoot aerial footage in some areas, so Chinese crews were sent aloft to record the required scenes, first on videotape and later—after approval from the Disney director in charge of the project—on film."

The narrator and host in the film was the character of Li Bai (aka Li Po), one of the greatest of Chinese poets from the 8th Century Tang Dynasty who spent much of his life traveling. Using this character helped to unify the many disparate sequences. In the film the voice of the character is portrayed by Keye Luke an artist and film actor best known for being the "Number One Son" in many Charlie Chan films and as the Chinatown shopkeeper Mr. Wing in *Gremlins* (1984).

Wonders of China also played in the World Premiere Circle-Vision theater in Tomorrowland at Disneyland from 1984 to 1996.

Skyleidoscope:
An Aerial Spectacular
(1985)

Originally Skyleidoscope was to be titled "Magical Rainbows". It was Disney Marketing that felt the name Skyleidoscope (a kaleidoscope of color filling the sky) was stronger.

Ron Logan, executive vice president of WDW Entertainment at the time, told me "Skyleidoscope was (Disney COO) Frank Wells' favorite show. He used to come out to the control booth about thirty minutes prior to show time and take a nap in the warm Florida sun until the show started."

The September 1985 issue of *Walt Disney World News* described the show with the following blurb:

> Each Saturday and Sunday this fall at 3 pm, the aerial spectacle of Skyleidoscope transforms the 45 acre World Showcase Lagoon into a colorful fantasy-land of purple dragons, exploding gumdrops, and whimsical flying machines as Epcot Center kicks off a giant celebration (that was to tie in with the 15th anniversary of Walt Disney World).

> It's a gala extravaganza of sea and sky wrapped in a kaleidoscope of magical rainbows made from silk, smoke, and sparkle. Set to a marvelous musical symphony, the 15 minute extravaganza features 60 flying, whirling, sailing objects of imagination and 80 aero-mariners.

> Dreamfinder, the famous character from Epcot Center's Journey into Imagination, directs his whimsical navy and air force from an 85 foot airship. Together they try to build magical rainbows but are thwarted by the invasion of winged dragons in the lagoon below.

> Calling on an entire fleet of candy-striped para-sails, speedy sea scooters, colorful sailboats and sea planes, Dreamfinder commands an exciting battle of fireworks and frenzy, until the monstrous dragons turn into harmless dragonflies. Only then can

Dreamfinder create rainbows so breathtaking that only seeing is believing.

This colorful daytime spectacular also included a bevy of dancers, musicians, singers and actors. It was so popular that it ran until August 1987 when a plane crash killing a pilot on a practice flight roughly an hour before a scheduled show closed it forever.

Originally, the show was just meant to run on Saturday and Sunday afternoons but was later expanded to Saturday through Wednesday and then every day during busy holiday periods. It packed the area around the World Showcase Lagoon much as the Illuminations fireworks nighttime display does today. WDW press releases described the new "sea and air" extravaganza as a "fairy tale come to life."

The mascots of Epcot Center that had been opened barely three years were Dreamfinder and his little dragon Figment who appeared in the attraction Journey Into Imagination and also as "walk-around" costumed characters. So, it was natural that the new show would showcase them.

Basically, in his huge blimp Dreamfinder was going to paint the sky in an array of colorful rainbows. However, he was disrupted in this cheerful pursuit by a bunch of evil Dragons known as "Ma and Pa" and their ten purplish "Dragonettes" who stirred up the lagoon to disrupt the show. (According to the narration the dragons were from the "black lagoon".)

The two sides did battle on the surface of the lagoon with sailboats, powerboats and hovercraft fitted into various colorful creatures until Dreamfinder triumphed over evil, accompanied by music, fireworks and a V-formation of brightly colored ultralight aircraft ("World Showcase Airforce") trailing streams of different colored smoke creating the effect of a rainbow.

According to Disney's promotional material, "The show turns ultra-light seaplanes and kits, jet skiers and speedboats, polkedol sailboats and airlifted saucers into purple-winged dragons, jet-powered sea shells, dragonfly-patrol planes and hang glider toys."

Illuminations: Reflections of Earth

(1999 – 2019)

Epcot tried several different nighttime fireworks shows including Carnival de Lumiere that debuted in October 1982 and A New World Fantasy that started in the summer of 1983. Finally, Laserphonic Fantasy in 1984 featuring music on synthesizers continued until the newest show in 1988.

In 1988, Illuminations premiered utilizing a full orchestra soundtrack that featured a celebration of the individual countries. Billed as "an international fantasy of music and light" the show featured classical music to accompany the effects. Holiday IllumiNations played during the holiday season instead of the regular show with suitable Christmas music.

For the new millennium, a new World Showcase Lagoon fireworks show called "IllumiNations: Reflections of Earth" created and directed by Don Dorsey premiered September 1999 and was rated by guests to Epcot as their most popular experience. There were several variations of the show over the decades and it ended in 2019 and was replaced by Epcot Forever.

For the show, nineteen natural gas torches were installed around the World Showcase lagoon to each represent the previous nineteen centuries with the final torch illuminating the new century coming out of the Earth Globe during the finale.

Roughly thirty percent more fireworks were added to the show, than in previous IllumiNations. For the new show, there were over 1,000 shells launched, producing some 2,400 effects. There were four fountain barges pumping 5,000 gallons per minute, along with three positioned lasers (Mexico, Canada, American Adventure) that produced a full rainbow of color. It took 67 computers working in forty locations to operate this show.

ACT 1 was entitled "Chaos" and captured the fiery early history of planet Earth. A shooting star explodes over the center of the lagoon, dancing fire and fountains shoot up like jets of lava, and huge gas flames of fire erupt into the air. The blackened inferno barge shot up forty-five feet tall propane gas flames.

ACT 2 was entitled "Order" and the Earth Globe took center stage. In this scene, color fireworks that were customized specifically for the show included Mint Green, Pumpkin Orange, Lavender and Lagoon Blue. The Earth Globe served as a massive video screen with hundreds of images showing the history of the Earth from animals, to primitive man, to exploration, to architectural wonders, to famous faces from history, including Walt Disney. The final image is of an astronaut, who sees the Earth in its true context: as "one place; one home to all".

The Earth Globe barge that was the centerpiece of the show was a sphere about twenty-eight feet high and weighing approximately 350,000 pounds which was the equivalent to the weight of about 150 midsize cars. It was the world's first spherical display system.

It was covered with LED (light emitting diode) video screens that represented the continents around the globe. The main structure of each petal of the sphere consists of four inch thick steel plates. The hydraulic system is capable of producing 650,000 pounds of force.

ACT III is entitled "Meaning", the show finale, concluding the evening with amazing fireworks and music.

The show was designed to tell the story of the planet Earth, and the link between the past and future. The Finale of IllumiNations:

> We go on, to the joy and through the tears...
> We go on, to DISCOVER new frontiers...
> Moving on, with the current of the years...
> We go on, moving forward now as one...
> Moving on, with a spirit born to run....
> Ever on, with each rising sun, to a new day...We Go On!

Epcot Parades

Tapestry of Nations Parade (1999 - 2001) Tapestry of Nations was selected as the theme for a parade to embrace an international audience and to reaffirm the World Showcase commitment as part of the Millenium celebration at the park.

Show director Gary Paben explained:

> A tapestry has many threads and our tapestry symbolically represents the diversity of planet Earth, and our hope for a better world woven with compassion, love, kindness and joy. When you weave all of these elements into it, you have a magnificent image, and that image represents the human spirit.

The forty huge puppet characters were designed by Michael Curry who also designed the puppets for the Broadway stage version of *The Lion King*. Each puppet weighed between eight and eighteen pounds and added an additional fifteen to eighteen feet in height to its puppeteer.

The impressionistically-styled puppets were not meant to represent any particular culture and included Aztec Man, Bird Man, Inverted (or Reverse) Marionette, Angel Girl, Wiggle Girl, Disc Man, Hammered Man and The Sprite.

The puppets were interspersed with fifteen identical rolling percussion units called Millennium Clocks that were 19 feet tall and 16 feet wide with drummers on each side.

In order to effectively control the time of the parade around the lengthy World Showcase Promenade walkway to roughly twenty minutes, three separate identical units were released simultaneously at different locations along the parade route.

One unit started from the area between the Millennium Village and the UK pavilion; another from between Morocco and Japan and the third from the gate between Germany and the Refreshment Outpost. Sometimes the route would be reversed and over the years were reduced to two processions and finally just one.

The parade began with the Sage of Time, who was represented by a stilt walker wearing a white robe with gold trim that had designs of timepieces and alchemy symbols as well as a headpiece resembling a sun with a face.

The music was composed by Gavin Greenaway, who also scored *IllumiNations 2000: Reflections of Earth*. The parade included the song *Celebrate the Future Hand in Hand*.

There were actually three versions of Tapestry of Nations, primarily with differences in the audio like changing the more serious narration of the Sage of Time into a more gentle interpretation and later incorporating the idea of dreams. Tapestry of Nations served as the theme of the 2000 Super Bowl XXXIV halftime show with the Sage of Time and huge puppets.

Tapestry of Dreams Parade (2001 – 2003). Because of its popularity, the parade was re-themed into the Tapestry of Dreams Parade and only traveled from Mexico to Morocco twice a day.

The Sage of Time was replaced by three Dream Seekers: Elfen (nature, magic, emotion), Cosmos (space, the universe, infinity) and Leonardo Columbus (discovery, invention and genius). The parade concept was re-themed to be a "visible dream" in which ideas, images, and emotions are evoked and the dreams of the guests, especially the children, are collected in the hope that they will spring to life.

The music (with additional contributions from Jonathon Barr) now featured new spoken introductions by the Dream Seekers and the voices of children speaking their dreams in many different languages. The parade also had a tribute to Walt Disney who it proclaimed was "...the greatest and most wonderful dreamer of all!"

Children would write their dreams down on a piece of paper and place them in the butterfly style nets of the Dreamkeepers as they harvested them as they passed by those along the parade route.

Disney's Hollywood Studios

Disney-MGM Studios opened May 1, 1989 dedicated to the Hollywood that never was but always will be. The park retained that name until 2008 when it was renamed Disney's Hollywood Studios that Disney indicated would only be a temporary placeholder but it has remained for over a decade.

Other things were not so permanent and faded from the park including the following that might be fondly remembered:

The Earffel Tower was a parody of the name of the famous Eiffel Tower in France. It was 130 feet high with a pair of 5,000 pound mouse ears. Movie studios used water towers for heating, cooling, and emergency uses. Most studios like Warner Brothers also used these towers as skyline billboards for their studio.

The one at the park was inspired by the working water tower built in 1939 at the Walt Disney Studios in Burbank and was really only visible on the Backlot Tour. The tower at the park tank was not designed to hold water. It was topped by a 32,000 pound Mouseketeer cap with each ear weighing almost 5,000 pounds. Measuring 28.5 feet in diameter, the hat size would be 342 3/8. The tower was removed in 2016 to make room for Toy Story Land.

The largest Hidden Mickey in the world disappeared as the park changed. Originally, an aerial view revealed the 330 foot wide face of Mickey Mouse, outlined by the wall that separated the production facilities from the theme park. Mickey's mouth was framed by Sunset Plaza, and his eyes and nose shaped by planters.

His left ear was formed by the distinctly colored rooftop of the Soundstage Restaurant with the 250 foot wide Echo Lake forming his right ear. When Sunset Boulevard opened in 1994 and the restaurant was re-roofed, Mickey lost an ear. Adding a huge Sorcerer's Hat in front of the Chinese Theater didn't help the image either.

The Monster Sound Show sponsored by Sony was an interactive experience where guests participated as sound effects artists recreating the effects of a horror comedy where a deranged butler played by Martin Short tries to get rid of an insurance salesman played by Chevy Chase.

It changed in 1997 to the ABC Sound Studio where guests now had to add sound effects to a clip from the animated *101 Dalmatians: The Series*. It then became *Sounds Dangerous* with Drew Carey in 1999.

The show was described by Disney as "while playing a undercover cop disguised as a security guard who bungles his first on-camera case, the hidden camera in his tie gets damaged, the video disappears and the theater is plunged into total darkness—leaving you to listen in as the hilarious mystery unfolds." It disappeared in 2011. The theater was then used for previews of upcoming Disney films.

Superstar Television had thirty guests chosen to re-enact scenes from one of several classic televisions shows from the 1960s to the 1980s including riding a horse in the opening credits of *Bonanza*, joining the cast of *Gilligan's Island* or *Golden Girls*, being a guest on Howard Cosell's *Sportsbreak* or chatting with Johnny Carson on the *Tonight Show* among other options.

SuperStar Television ran until 1998. It was replaced by Doug Live!, which debuted in 1999 and ended in 2001. The theater then hosted the American Idol Experience beginning in 2009. In 2015, a Frozen Sing-Along show took over what is now known as the Hyperion Theater.

The Sorcerer Hat

(2001 – 2015)

The Sorcerer Hat took up residence in front of the Chinese Theater on September 28, 2001. The public and cast members were assured that the structure was temporary as part of the 100 Years of Magic celebration but it remained in place until 2015.

It was meant to be a clear icon to identify the park on merchandising and marketing materials like Cinderella Castle, Spaceship Earth and the Tree of Life at the other three parks.

The hat towered at the end of Hollywood Boulevard and was inspired by a segment in the Disney animated feature film *Fantasia* (1940) in which Mickey Mouse who was a sorcerer apprentice steals the hat and disaster ensues. The hat represented "the magic of show business and the entertainment wizardry of Disney," according to Disney publicity materials and tied-in with the park's theme of Hollywood in the 1940s.

Here are the official figures for the composite fiberglass hat when it was originally constructed. It took nine months to build.

- Hat Height — The hat itself was 100 feet tall. Since it was resting atop the ears and canted to the side, the summit of the icon was 122 feet.

- Icon Weight – 156 tons

- Hat Weight (the brim and hat only, excluding the ears and support structure) – 27 tons

- Hat Size (as wardrobe) – The hat is a size 605 and 7/8

- Mickey Size (if he were to wear it) – For a proportional perspective, Mickey, wearing this hat, would be 350 feet tall. (Based on scaling the real-life costumed characters in the park.)

- Hat Paint (Chameleon Paint) – The hat is painted with a custom paint technique called "chameleon paint" that causes the hat to shift in color as guests move closer and around it. Disney used enough of this "automotive type paint" to cover 500 Cadillacs.

- Mickey Ears (Light Ribbon) – The faces of the ears were new special effect called "Light Ribbons" (by Walt Disney Imagineering).
- The ears appear to change colors, surface shapes and sparkle with internal pixie dust lighting.
- 91 panels for the hat
- 18 sections for the brim
- 18 spirals
- 6 stars
- 2 moons
- 13 total air vents
- 13,493 bolts holding the hat together
- 26,986 washers
- 17,000 feet (or 57 football fields) of underground utility piping
- Hat interior space = 59,458 cubic feet
- Hat can hold 444,744 gallons of water
- Ring Beam = 56-1/2 feet in diameter

During the 100 Years of Magic celebration, there were interactive kiosks located underneath the hat where guests were encouraged to learn more about the life and career of Walt Disney. After the celebration, the kiosks were removed and the area was converted into a pin-selling location since the retail division of the Disney Company had shouldered the cost for building it in the first place.

On April 11, 2003, a new sculpture, replacing the 100 Years of Magic Celebration logo under the Sorcerer Mickey Icon debuted. This permanent sculpture featured gold ribbons decorated with silver stars and was located adjacent to a merchandise venue under the Sorcerer Mickey Hat Icon.

Originally the hat was supposed to have been placed outside the park entrance.. At one time it was proposed to be the building to house the One Man's Dream attraction but it was determined it would be less expensive to convert an existing building. Another version would have had Mickey's ears as working ferris wheels, with the hat as the entrance to the attraction.

The Great Movie Ride
(1989 – 2017)

Boarding theater style ride vehicles, guests journeyed from a soundstage into re-creations of twelve classic movie scenes populated by audio-animatronics figures.

The Great Movie Ride attraction was to have had live celebrity impersonators interacting with the guests but it was decided that audio-animatronics figures would not only be more cost-effective, but would provide a more consistent show experience for guests.

Imagineers wined and dined actor Gene Kelly before showing him his doppelganger for the ride so that Kelly signed off immediately for the scene from *Singin' in the Rain* (1952). When the ride first debuted, Kelly's open umbrella caused water to occasionally splatter off of it onto the guests.

Actor James Cagney's family was unhappy with his attire in the gangster scene from his classic film *Public Enemy* (1931) so they gave the Imagineers one of Cagney's actual tuxedos so he would appear more "classy".

The prop newspapers scattered around the Patrick J. Ryan's bar that cannot be seen clearly by the guests are actually copies of the local Florida paper, the *Orlando Sentinel*. The puddles on the ground are not real liquid and often accumulate dust and need to be wiped during maintenance as do the "horse puddles" in the Western scene.

Liza Minnelli, the daughter of actress Judy Garland, supplies the voice for the character of Dorothy in the *Wizard of Oz* (1939) scene. Ingrid Bergman does not speak in the *Casablanca* (1942) scene because her family would not give permission to use her voice. Actor Humphrey Bogart was shorter than Bergman in real life but his figure is taller in the attraction.

John Wayne's voice was impersonated by actor Doug McClure. When he was alive, Wayne had heard McClure impersonating him and apparently approved of it. When the ride originally opened, the figure did wear the real belt buckle that the actor wore in the movie *Red River* (1948). However, as soon as that information became public knowledge, it was stolen and a replica took its place.

The little band that the Wayne figure wears on his right wrist was one that Wayne was given for good luck when he visited Vietnam and that remained for the duration of the attraction.

The cards on the floor by the Clint Eastwood figure originally had numbers on them, but during a rehab were changed out to cards with just the suits, which were more authentic to the time period. Eastwood's figure does not represent a specific scene from any of his films. The figure was a next-to-last-minute replacement for actor Lee Marvin, when his family refused to authorize his Oscar winning portrayal of a gunfighter sitting on a tipsy horse from the comedy *Cat Ballou* (1965).

Actress Maureen O'Sullivan who played Jane in the movie *Tarzan the Ape Man* (1932) did come to Orlando and got a picture taken with her audio-animatronics double on the elephant.

When her figure was built in California and ready to be shipped to Florida, it was wrapped in clear plastic and completely unclothed (since the clothes would be added when the figure was installed so that they would hang properly) and many people made unnecessary trips to the loading dock just to check it out.

In June 2015, the attraction saw many changes with the new sponsorship of Turner Classic Movies including having movie historian Robert Osborne not only host a longer pre-show film but also narrate the ride. In addition, there was a different movie montage as the finale. The attraction was replaced by Mickey & Minnie's Runaway Railway that opened in 2020.

Film Production

The new Disney MGM Studios theme park when it opened in 1989 was touted as an actual production facility where television shows, movies, and animated films would be made. The local media proclaimed that the opening would herald the beginning of Hollywood East.

Unfortunately, due to lack of facilities, materials, personnel, post-production bays, and, more importantly, support (for example, if something broke in Hollywood, a quick call across town would have a replacement there no later than that same afternoon, but, in Florida, it might take several days to have it shipped from somewhere else in the country), it didn't happen.

TV shows, like *Wheel of Fortune*, brought their own trucks and equipment to edit and upload the shows for broadcast later in the same day they were shot, rather than pay the exorbitant rental fees being charged by Disney for the same limited facilities.

In addition, producers had to fly their talent out from Hollywood and pay for upscale housing and transportation, causing a significant increase in the budget. In the early years, the state of Florida helped out on compensating some of those additional costs in the hopes of encouraging more film production to come to the state to boost the local economy.

With a production budget of three and a half million dollars, *Splash Too* (1988), a made-for television sequel to the popular Disney live action movie *Splash*, was the first movie to be filmed at the new complex.

The production facilities at Disney MGM Studios opened in June of 1988, roughly a year before the park, and projects like *Win, Lose or Draw*, *Siskel & Ebert*, a Carol Burnett special, *Good Morning Miss Bliss* (a precursor to *Saved by the Bell*, with Hayley Mills), the first season of the syndicated *Superboy* (1988), gameshow *Remote Control* (MTV), and the *New Mickey Mouse Club* began filming there.

Over the early years, other productions that filmed, or partially filmed, at the park included *Ernest Saves Christmas* (1988 with Vern's house a façade on Residential Street on the backlot); *Newsies* (1992); *Sheena (Queen of the Jungle)* with Gena Lee Nolin (2000); *From the Earth to the Moon* (1998 HBO mini-series from Ron Howard and Tom Hanks pumping roughly $37 million dollars into the local economy); *Teen Win, Lose or Draw*; and *Adventures in Wonderland*; as well as tapings for *World Championship Wrestling*.

Thunder in Paradise (1994 with Chris Lemmon and Hulk Hogan) employed some local Central Florida actors and production was shot at Disney's Grand Floridian Resort and Spa, as well at Disney's Old Key West Resort, Fort Wilderness Resort and Campground, and even Epcot (where the Morocco pavilion was the backdrop for at least two episodes).

Disney-MGM Studios had less than half the physical space as its nearby competitor Universal and found some productions moving to that larger venue.

To expand its array of services, the studio signed a five-year deal with Lightpoint Entertainment Inc., a digital effects company that specialized in 3-D animation to assist with the syndicated television series *Mortal Kombat Conquest* (that made use of the China and Morocco pavilions at World Showcase).

When the State of Florida ended its compensation package for film companies, the productions started going to other states. In addition, the challenges of doing production from limited space to equipment issues also contributed greatly to the decision to close down the Central Florida production units.

The soundstages were converted for use for the Pixar Place expansion.

Back To Neverland
(1989 – 2003)

The Magic of Disney Animation pavilion featured a short film entitled *Back to Neverland*.

In the film, distinguished news commentator Walter Cronkite turns imaginative comedian Robin Williams into an animated character, one of the little Lost Boys from Disney's animated feature film *Peter Pan* (1953), to demonstrate the different steps in animation.

The entire pavilion was outsourced to Bob Rogers and BRC Imagination Arts who had struggled on different variations to explain the process of animation for nine months when director Jerry Rees was brought in to provide a new perspective.

Rees suggested using the authority of famed newscaster Walter Cronkite presenting the facts to play as counterpoint against the unbridled childlike enthusiasm of comedian Robin Williams for animation.

It turned out that Williams was a huge fan of Cronkite and ironically, Cronkite was a fan of Williams and they really wanted to work together.

To help sell the project to the performers as well as Eisner, Rees brought in famed voice artist Corey Burton who did spot on imitations of both of them for a scratch track (a rough test before professional voices are cast). In fact, when Eisner heard it, he thought it was them. Burton was cast as the voice of Captain Hook.

Rees assured Robin that he was free to improv lines as long as he got the sense of what was needed to be communicated and landed on the lines that were Cronkite's cues.

Rees recalled:

> He gave us a wealth of material. Especially during the metamorphosis scene. That could have been over ten minutes just by itself. We had to be brutal to edit that segment.

Animator Bruce Smith (who had just finished doing animation on the 1988 *Who Framed Roger Rabbit)* had done some test animation of Robin's character because the voice work had been recorded earlier and flipped it for him when we shot the live action at the Raleigh stages in Hollywood:

> Robin was just delighted with it. He thought it was magical that it had his personality. When we were filming the live action scenes, I invited the animators to come and hang out and Robin was very respectful and gracious with them.

Animator Mark Kausler recalled:

> Jerry Rees was also directing the live action as well as the animation. He knew the Peter Pan feature backwards and forwards, knew every Frank Thomas, Ollie Johnston and Woolie Reitherman scene. We studied a lot of the *Peter Pan* feature frame-by-frame with Jerry.

> We all took turns animating all the characters. I did a nice close shot of Robin and Tinker Bell that I enjoyed. We were on a tight deadline, so we all pitched in and did any scenes that came our way.

Frans Vischer animated the improvisational sequence in which Robin's character swiftly changed into many forms, including even Walter Cronkite. The line during the metamorphosis scene where Robin transforms into Mickey Mouse and gleefully proclaims "I'm a corporate symbol" was written by Steve Moore. It stayed in the final cut because Robin loved it so much.

After seeing this short film, co-director of *Aladdin* (1992) John Musker told Rees that he and co-director Ron Clements wrote the part of the Genie specifically for Robin. As a tribute, at the end of the animated feature, the Genie appears in the same yellow Hawaiian shirt and Goofy hat that Robin wore in the live action beginning of *Back to Neverland.*

The film was replaced in 2003 with one of Mushu the dragon from *Mulan* (1998) supplying updated information on the current process of animation.

Hidden Handprints

(1989 – 2015)

On May 1, 1989, the Disney MGM Studios officially opened with a dedication ceremony led by then CEO Michael Eisner. However, not long afterwards on that same day, there was another dedication ceremony in front of The Magic of Disney Animation building.

Roy E. Disney talked at a podium set up in the front of the attraction where he emphasized that hand drawn animation was really the focal point of the Walt Disney Company. He continued to talk about the fact that animation was the start of the Disney Company and that with the newly opened Disney Feature Animation Studio Florida "a new day for animation will be dawning".

The animated feature film *The Little Mermaid* would debut in November, just six months later, proving Roy absolutely correct.

Joining in the dedication were several Disney Legends who had made significant contributions to animation: Frank Thomas, Ollie Johnston, Ward Kimball, Marc Davis, Ken O'Connor and Ken Anderson. O' Connor, who was primarily known for his work on backgrounds in Disney animated films, was there because he had worked as a consultant on the *Back to Neverland* short film being shown in the pavilion.

The one snag in the ceremony was a literal snag as the cover over the elaborate animation film strip sculpture at the front of the building did indeed get caught on a pointy outcropping of the sculpture. Amid the fanfare, releasing of balloons and applause, several Disney executives struggled in a tug of war to release the red cover from its entanglement and eventually succeeded.

There was also a ceremony where these six animation legends put their handprints and autographs into cement blocks to be placed in an alcove of the outdoor animation courtyard inside the building.

The original intention was that there were would two legends to one block as demonstrated on the one featuring Frank Thomas and Ollie Johnston, longtime friends as well as co-workers. Their hands and signatures are neatly and symmetrically imprinted, along with an impression of their pencils. This was how all the blocks were to look.

However, another block features three handprints and signatures: Marc Davis, Ken Anderson and Ken O'Connor, once again with impressions of their drawing pencils. Yet, Anderson's signature seems crowded and his last name curves downward as if squeezed for space or an afterthought.

The secret is clear on the final block knowing the behavior of the exuberant Ward Kimball, an extrovert known for being an unpredictable maverick. Not only did he make sure his pencil was broken before being imprinted unlike his fellow legends, he also spread his fingers wide so he could make a second impression and close examination will reveal that he has six fingers on each hand, something that most guests missed at a casual glance.

Also, in a fit of high spirits, he filled the bottom half of the block with a quick drawing of Mickey Mouse's head in the space that was going to be filled by Ken Anderson. Who would be so bold as to wipe out a Mickey Mouse drawing by the legendary Kimball? Apparently, no one. So Anderson squeezed in to a space on another block.

Those hidden handprints were available for every DHS guest to enjoy until they were removed when the Star Wars Launch Bay opened on December 1, 2015.

One Man's Dream
(2001 – 2015)

One Man's Dream was opened as part of the year-long 100 Years of Magic: Share a Dream Come True event that was to kick off on Walt Disney World's 30th anniversary on October 1, 2001, and be a spectacular celebration of the 100th anniversary of the birth of Walt Disney.

I interviewed Imagineering Senior Show Producer Roger Holzberg in 2001:

> One Man's Dream will enable guests to journey into Walt's imagination and that is why the pathway flows back and forth like a wave. His imagination still speaks loudly to the child in us all.

> Guests' footsteps will set into play a remarkable collection of rarely-heard audio commentary by Walt himself. The attraction will culminate in an inspiring and emotional fifteen minute film about a man who was never crushed by failure, and never spoiled by success.

> When we were researching the attraction, we found that many of our guests under the age of 15 did not know Walt Disney was a real person. They thought it was just the name of the company. We want to present the idea that Walt was an individual, not an icon. This tells the story of Walt the man, and we hope that guests will be moved by the scope of his imagination, what he accomplished, and what he inspired.

Disney Archivist Dave Smith supervised the collection and transportation of more than 400 items that arrived at Walt Disney World via Federal Express from California on an Airbus A300 designated the "Spirit of Imagination". The coast-to-coat delivery took just a few hours on June 29, 2001.

The attraction was a walk-through exhibit with the curving pathway underneath the Guests' feet reflecting the different decades of Walt's life, beginning with a yellow brick road that transformed into a wooden path in the Marceline, Missouri, era and linoleum in the 1950s. Overhead was a swirling banner that listed what was happening in the world during the same time period, along with appropriate photos.

Near many of the exhibits were "Connection Cards" that connected what was seen like Walt dressing up as President Lincoln in grammar school with the Audio-Animatronics Lincoln figure for the 1964 New York's World Fair later in the attraction.

Originally Disney CEO Michael Eisner was the narrator for the final film, but when he exited the Disney Company in 2005, he was replaced by Disneyland 50th Anniversary Ambassador, actress Julie Andrews, reading the same script. A lot of Walt's voice-over came from the recorded interviews he did with *Saturday Evening Post* writer Pete Martin in June and July 1956.

The exhibit was briefly closed and rehabbed (with such things as the swirling timeline banner removed) and reopened in March 2009 with some new items from the Disney Archives and now sponsored by D23, in hopes of nudging true Disney fans into joining that organization.

From August 16 to November 2, 2010, the attraction received another refurbishment that removed some of the displays and added new ones in their place including a final section entitled "The Legacy Continues" to showcase more recent achievements. The interior color palette was changed as well.

Originally meant just to last the eighteen months of the original celebration, Disney found that it would be too expensive to dismantle Walt's Working Office and ship it back to California as well as the operational need to have another attraction open especially during all the construction for Star Wars Land and Toy Story Land.

Changes in One Man's Dream

(2001 -2015)

Not all of the artifacts that originally appeared in the One Man's Dream attraction were owned by the Disney Company. Some were borrowed from other sources and, after the first year, were returned to the owners with replicas often taking their place.

In one of the first display cases it was implied that it was Walt's elementary school desk from Marceline's Park School but that was not true. The desk belonged to Marceline, Missouri, that displays it there under plexiglass during the year at the school and sometimes at Walt Disney's Hometown Museum.

When the exhibit opened, the desk was on loan to the Ronald Reagan Presidential Library and Museum for its exhibit, *Walt Disney: The Man and His Magic* (May 13-September 4, 2001) and once it was finished there, it was returned to Marceline because it was larger than the display case in the One Man's Dream exhibit.

Also in the Reagan exhibit was the famous Oscar and seven little Oscar statuettes given to Walt for *Snow White and the Seven Dwarfs* (1937). That icon did make its way to One Man's Dream to sit on top of Walt's actual office desk from the Hyperion Studios, but when the Walt Disney Family Museum opened in 2009, the Disney family took it back since it was their personal property. It is now displayed at that San Francisco location.

When the exhibit opened that was indeed an authentic animation desk in the display that was on loan from the Los Angeles Natural History Museum. Walt himself donated the animation stand to the museum in 1938 and claimed that he had used that very stand for the production of *Steamboat Willie* (1928) after it had been upgraded from being used on the Alice Comedies. It was only on loan for the celebration, so it had to be returned and a replica created to take its place.

Originally, the exhibit had the actual model (with some minor restoration) of Sleeping Beauty Castle done by Imagineer Fred Joerger, but when Disneyland celebrated its 50th anniversary in 2005, the real model was shipped back for a display at Disneyland. Once again, a replica took its place in Orlando.

When the attraction first opened, guests were able to view, up-close, the white dress worn by actress Julie Andrews in *Mary Poppins* (1964). However, after a few years, an examination revealed that the heat, humidty and light were damaging the dress despite all precautions so it was replaced with the suit worn by actor Fred MacMurray in the feature film *Bon Voyage* (1962).

The multiplane camera was not the real one but a small replica. Three original Disney multiplane cameras still survive. One is at the Burbank Studios in the lobby of the Disney Archives, another one is at the Walt Disney Family Museum in San Francisco, and the third is at the Art of Disney Animation attraction in Disneyland Paris.

In 2009, Disney Archivist Becky Cline found in the Disney studio prop department two of the trunks used personally by Walt on his travels. One of them was placed by his desk in the attraction.

Walt's Working Office was removed from the exhibit and re-installed at the Disney Studio in Burbank in 2015. Using old photos as a guide, archivists faithfully restored the space as part of the studio's 75th anniversary in Burbank and even included the ashtrays and matchbooks.

Walt's Bust
(1993 – 2016)

The Television Academy of Arts and Sciences established a Hall of Fame in 1984 to recognize extraordinary contributions to television and specifically honor particular individuals. The third year ceremony in 1986 inducted Walt Disney whose wife Lillian accepted the award.

In May 1991, when the Academy moved to its current headquarters, on the corner of Magnolia and Lankershim boulevards in North Hollywood, California, it installed the Hall of Fame Plaza, an outdoor exhibit of statuary and wall sculptures honoring past inductees.

Walt Disney's bust was added in a 1993 ceremony done by Hall of Fame Chairman Edgar Scherick: "Walt Disney understood the power of television perhaps better than anyone. He used it to create a national fascination with his new theme park. He used television to educate and enlighten and became one of the most loved and trusted individuals in America as we welcomed him into our living rooms."

The bronze bust of Walt Disney was the work of Disney Legend Blaine Gibson who sculpted the piece in 1991 and signed it on the back of the base as "B. Gibson 1991."

While working at Imagineering, Gibson ended up sculpting everything from Indian chiefs to mermaids to bathing elephants to, eventually, President Lincoln, Haunted Mansion ghosts, and blood-thirsty pirates—among just a few of his many accomplishments.

In 1962, at the urging of his WED Imagineering supervisor, Richard "Dick" Irvine, Gibson sculpted a bust of Walt Disney as a "thank you" gift for Walt. Gibson now claims he was tired, working on the project late at night, and that the foundry work was not very good and he couldn't quite control what he wanted.

When he presented it to Walt, Gibson claimed that Walt said, "What am I going to do with this? Statues are for dead people!"

Gibson wanted to destroy the bust and replace it with another, but it was kept at WED for awhile and then at RETLAW, the company owned by Walt himself. Gibson said that Walt was so animated in real life and constantly shifting in appearance that it was hard to capture a frozen moment in time. Gibson pulled out his old model, done while Walt was alive, and used it as a reference for the new bust.

On May 6, 1993, actress and producer Mary Tyler Moore (who had been inducted the same year as Walt into the Hall of Fame) joined a costumed Mickey Mouse (wearing a tuxedo and holding an oversized jackhammer) for a groundbreaking ceremony at the Disney MGM Studios for a smaller replica of the fabled Hall of Fame Plaza. The Disney version of the plaza was located to the side of what is now called the Hyperion Theater.

It was CEO Michael Eisner's intent that each fall, television legends and industry executives would gather at the location to honor present and former inductees.

The plaza itself was unveiled on November 20, 1993. Bronze busts of Carol Burnett, Sid Caesar, Bill Cosby (who was removed in 2015 because of negative publicity), Mary Tyler Moore, Red Skelton, Danny Thomas, Milton Berle and of course, Walt Disney, were in place for photo opportunities.

In late September 2016, walls went up around the Academy of Television Arts and Sciences (ATAS) Hall of Fame Plaza without warning in preparation for its removal that was confirmed by Disney officially in early October. Disney has stated that all the busts were shipped back to ATAS in North Hollywood because it is considered their property.

Lights, Motors, Action!
(2005 – 2016)

Lights, Motors, Action! was a stunt show that opened at Disney MGM Studio in May 2005. It was based on the Disney Studio Parks' *Moteurs... Action! Stunt Show Spectacular* in Paris that had been running since 2002.

Disney promoted the show as "Experience the excitement as cars accelerate towards each other and swerve away at the last second, motorcycles smash through windows, Jet Skis leap out of the water, a stunt person falls off a 5-story building and massive fireballs explode in the air. See all of these Hollywood-style stunts performed live, right before your disbelieving eyes!"

The roughly thirty-five minute show showed off the skills of professional stunt drivers in more than forty automobiles executing a series of choreographed 180 and 360 degree spins and jumps sometimes in the middle of controlled explosions that rattled the seats of the guests sitting in the grandstand.

The stunts were filmed in real-time by cameras (in addition to pre-recorded material). These segments were shown to the audience on overhead billboard television screens for a close-up look at the action, stunt work and pyrotechnics. The scenes also demonstrated on how different angles are used to disguise certain things or enhance the special effects.

Originally, the show had an intermission appearance by Herbie, the Love Bug who would split into two sections. He was later replaced in 2011 by race car Lightning McQueen from *Cars* (2006). The show also included a Jetski segment that was not in the Paris show.

The rest of the show had only minor revisions during its eleven years of performances.

The premise of the full-throttle, high-octane show was that the 177,000 square foot, 5,000 seat stadium is a movie set for a spy movie where the hero must deliver a special secret envelope while evading the bad guys who are in pursuit.

The set was designed to resemble the Villefranche-sur-Mer Mediterranean village in the south of France. It was such a large venue that half of the Studio Backlot Tour had to be demolished including Residential Street that featured facades of houses used in film and television shows.

The "hero" car for the show was custom built while the villainous pursuit cars were Opel Corsa D cars. The hero cars were all painted red while the pursuit cars were painted black so that guests could clearly tell the difference. Each car got a new set of tires after every show.

The main hero car had two variations. One of which had the body shell installed backwards so it appeared to be driving in reverse. Another had a section bolted on the outside facing away from the audience so it appeared it was driving itself.

There was no pre-show other than some music and trivia games shown on the big screens. The show began with several scenes supposedly shot for the spy thriller to give the audience a sense of context for what they were about to see.

Because it was a stunt show, despite all the precautions, accidents did happen. In 2014, the hero car collided with the metal support bar on the truck/ramp, tearing off a large portion of the hero car's body work. The driver was able to bring the stunt car to a complete stop and exit the vehicle safely.

To make way for Star Wars Land and Toy Story Land, Lights, Motors, Action! gave it's last performance on April 2, 2016, after which time demolition quickly began.

Walt's Plane

(1993 – 2016)

Over the years, there were actually three Walt Disney Company planes:

- Queen Air (Beechcraft) 2/63 - 7/65
- King Air (Beechcraft) 1965 – 1967
- Gulfstream (Grumman) bought in 1963 and put in service 5/64, retired to WDW 10/8/92 where it was put on display until 2016.

The FAA gave the Disney planes special call letters: N234MM--the N denotes a plane, and the MM is short of Mickey Mouse. All three planes had the same designation.

Walt had his own jump seat on the Gulfstream behind the cockpit, with an altimeter and air speed indicator on the wall next to the seat, and a telephone direct to the pilot. Walt contributed to the plane's interior design, and his wife, Lillian assisted in selecting materials and colors.

Walt had postcards of a photo of the interior produced to give as a memento to those who flew on the plane. Although Walt never acquired a pilot's license, he sometimes took over the plane's controls for brief periods on long flights.

Walt used the planes, not just for quick transportation across the country, but for checking out the available acreage in Florida for a theme park. After work in Florida began, the Gulfstream ferried Disney executives back and forth to the East Coast, and it was used for promotional tours for new Disney movies and for theme park promotions.

The plane also flew Disney characters on goodwill tours and visits to children's hospitals around the United States. An estimated 83,000 passengers (some of whom were given a special certificate acknowledging their flight) flew aboard the plane, including

Disney personnel and celebrities. Disney fans can catch a quick glimpse of the plane in the live action films *The Computer Wore Tennis Shoes* (1969) and *Now You See Him, Now You Don't* (1972).

Disney Archivist Dave Smith shared this personal anecdote about flying on "The Mouse" with me:

> I remember going on trips to Florida, where it took several hours to fly in the Mouse; you could do it two hours shorter in a commercial airliner. On return flights, with headwinds, they sometimes had to stop to refuel, even though it had long-range fuel capability for transcontinental travel.

When the plane was finally retired from service in October 8, 1992, it was flown to Walt Disney World to be displayed on the backlot tour at the Disney MGM Studios.

The STOLport airport area near the Magic Kingdom was considered unsafe and too small to use. So the corporate plane landed instead on World Drive (which had been completely shut down prior to the arrival) and was towed to the movie theme park. The interior was gutted so that it would never fly again and it was prepared to be included on the backstage tour experience.

It spent many years beginning in 1993 as an exhibit on the backlot tour in the green area behind Residential Street. When the area was converted into the Lights, Motors, Action! attraction, it was relocated to behind the bleacher seating where guests could still view it as they entered into the venue.

When the area was needed for Star Wars: Galaxy's Edge, the plane was removed in 2016. In March 2018, the plane was located, thanks to aerial photography done by Nearmap, over a restricted backstage area near the water treatment plant off of Western Way.

The plane was completely encircled by a number of barricades. Interestingly, the plane had been repainted complete with the original big orange stripe. It remains there today as evidenced by aerial photography.

Catastrophe Canyon

(1989 – 2014)

The Universal Studio Hollywood Backlot Tram Tour featured many special effects that delighted guests including a simulation of an earthquake on a soundstage designed to look like a "hot movie set" of a San Francisco subway station. Unexpectedly, the closed set sprung to life.

During that experience the tram shook, a burning gasoline truck collapsed through the roof, multiple fire and spark effects danced on the set, a derailing subway train suddenly crashed into the scene, and a flood of water rushed toward the guests. And then everything would re-set to reveal how movies make their magic.

When Disney MGM Studios designed a backlot tram tour they installed a very similar experience called Catastrophe Canyon.

The tram tour survived for twenty five years despite several modifications over the decades from the walking part of the tour becoming a different attraction entirely called Backstage Pass, the complete removal of Residential Street in 2003 for the installation of Lights, Motors, Action! Stunt Show to the live tour guides being replaced by a precorded spiel in 2008.

The original intent of the park was to provide guests with a behind-the-scenes glimpse at how films and television shows were made. The park's brocheure described Catastophe Canyon as "A perilous journey through a unique outdoor set. You'll experience amazing artificial disasters that seem real enough in the movies, but even more impressive up close".

After leaving the boneyard, guests were told that they would be entering a "live" movie set while the cast and crew were on break. The tram would then slowly move into an enclosed area known as Catastrophe Canyon, a mountainous area with an imposing fuel truck.

When the tram stops to give guests a better look, suddenly the set springs to life. An earthquake shakes the tram and causes the fuel truck to explode, sending a fire ball into the air. Then a flood of water comes rushing down from the top of the canyon and from the overhang above the tram.

When the earthquake and the water dwindle, the set would then begin to miracleously re-set for the next tram. The tram then traveled behind the area where the host told how the water and fire effects were accomplished.

While conceived by the Imagineers, the attraction was actually outsourced to Sequoia Creative in Sun Valley, California that was co-founded by former Imagineer Bob Gurr who was brought in to manufacture and install the attraction. The Imagineers had originally wanted a collapsing railroad bridge with some railroad oil tanker cars getting knocked into a sea of flames when a flash flood collapses the bridge.

That theatrical scene proved to be much too expensive so Gurr suggested forgetting about the bridge and the railroad since it wouldn't be of much interest to children. Instead he offered the idea of a highway gasoline tanker truck and to put it slightly higher than the guests' line of sight so it would seem to slide part way off the road toward the tram while roaring in flame. Gurr located an old worn-out diesel tractor and tanker for only $3,000 so it didn't need to be completely built and saved Disney big bucks.

A version of the attraction was installed at the Walt Disney Studios Park in Paris for its backlot tour in 2002. The final day of the attraction at DHS was September 27, 2014 and at DHS in 2016 Catastrophe Canyon was completely demolished to make room for Star Wars: Galaxy's Edge.

Honey, I Shrunk the Kids: Movie Set Adventure Playground
(1990 - 2016)

Honey, I Shrunk the Kids (1989) was a popular Disney live action movie about inventor Wayne Szalinski (Rick Moranis) who accidentally shrinks his own kids as well as his next door neighbor's children to a quarter of an inch high with his shrinking machine and also accidentally throws them outside with the trash and they must make their way through the backyard back to the house.

The high grossing film spawned two sequels and a television series as well as several attractions at Disney theme parks. On the Disney MGM Backlot walking tour, originally guests could get a chance to hang on to a giant bee from the film with a blue screen in the background as part of a demonstration of special effects.

The most prominent attraction was Epcot's 4-D attraction sponsored by Kodak called *Honey, I Shrunk the Audience* (1994 -2010) where at an awards show Szalinski temporarily shrinks the entire theater to the size of a shoebox. The attraction was later installed in Disneyland, Tokyo Disneyland and Disneyland Paris. All of them closed in 2010.

Honey, I Shrunk the Kids: Movie Set Adventure was also sponsored by Kodak for its first twenty years and the attraction was promoted as Honey, I Shrunk the Kids Play Set Adventure on the movie marquee on Streets of America that led into the entrance for the attraction but not on the official literature.

Disney described the attraction as "This interactive kids' playground sets the scene with larger-than-life props from the hit movie. Scale the Everest of anthills, crawl inside a discarded LEGO brick, and dodge the spritz from the biggest leaky garden hose you've ever seen."

Outside the attraction, guests saw the following posted notice: "This imaginative playground is best enjoyed by children 10 and under. We ask adults to shrink down with young children and supervise them on this exciting adventure. We urge you to exercise caution while climbing, sliding and exploring. Please use the pathways as they were carved out for your safety by adventurers before you. Remember: You are about to become the size of ant!"

Basically this 11,000 square foot themed area built roughly a year after the release of the original film opened in December 1990 and suggested that guests had been somehow shrunk down to roughly the size of an ant and have found themselves in the Szalinski backyard. The backyard is filled with thirty foot tall blades of grass, oversized Tinker Toy pieces, a huge can of Play Doh, a Super Soaker and many other objects both from the film but also new items as well.

There was a fifty-two foot long leaking water hose that sprayed sproadically, forty-foot tall bumblebees, a spider web that was a maze made out of climbing ropes, enormous breakfast cereal in "O" shapes to suggest *Cheerios*, a giant dog nose that issued a growling sound and sprayed a mist from its nostrils, jumbo plant-root mazes, a Kodak film canister that doubled as a children's slide, an explorable anthill and even an oversized ant with a saddle that guests could get on for photo opportunities.

Cast members were stationed at the entrance and exit so young chidlren could not enter or leave without a parent.

The playground was closed in 2016 to provide room for Star Wars: Galaxy's Edge.

Mermaid Statue
(1989 – 2016)

Near the Studio Catering Company quick serve restaurant and the bathrooms was a statue that was there since the park first opened in 1989 and was removed in 2016 to make way for Star Wars: Galaxy's Edge.

It depicts a classic demure mermaid sitting in a curved platform supported by four dolphins who are spouting water. The fountain was a prop from the Disney live action film *Splash* (1984).

Splash may not seem a significant enough film to be enshrined at Disney Hollywood Studios but it was the first film made by the new Touchstone division of Disney films that was created for movies that might have content not appropriate for a general Disney audience.

The film was a huge financial success. Made on a budget of eight million dollars, it grossed over six million dollars on just its opening weekend and went on to be the tenth highest grossing film of the year.

Directed by Ron Howard, the film recounts the story of Allen Bauer (Tom Hanks, in the first film where he received top billing) and his encounter with a mermaid named Madison (Daryl Hannah), and how it changed his life.

The beach where Tom Hanks encounters the mermaid was filmed at Castaway Cay (then known as Gorda Cay). According to legend, Ariel in *The Little Mermaid* (1989) was originally going to be blonde but was made a redhead to distinguish her from the blonde Madison.

The plaque by the statue stated:

SPLASH 1984.

This mermaid was Madison's gift to Allen. Although it appears to be made of brass and stone, it was fabricated entirely out of fiberglass at the Walt Disney Studios Scenic Shop.

The molds used to produce the mermaid and dolphins were originally created for ice sculptures seen in the Walt Disney Productions' film *Herbie Goes Bananas* (1980).

Splash was a favorite film of then CEO Michael Eisner and he green-lit a sequel called *Splash Too* with an entirely new cast and filmed for roughly three million dollars. It was the very first film to be completely filmed at the new Disney MGM Studios and was released in 1988.

Howard told Marilyn Beck of the *Chicago Tribune* newspaper on February 28, 1985:

> Because of the urgency Michael Eisner has placed on *Splash Too*, I'll limit myself to co-producing it with Brian Glazer. It will not be a copy-cat sequel. They will come back to land, but there will still be plenty of underwater action.

Eisner hoped the sequel would spin off into a popular television series which is another reason for the statue to be featured so prominently at the theme park. Unfortunately, the sequel didn't have the same impact critically or financially as the original.

Besides putting the statue in the park, Eisner intended that in 1989 at the now-extinct Pleasure Island there would be a sunken bar nightclub called Madison's Dive filled with sailors telling tall fish tales including about an elusive mermaid who would occasionally swim by one of the windows below sea level.

Some of the effects including the sinking ship in the bottle were later incorporated into the extinct Adventurers Club. Madison's Dive would have been built on a pier that jutted out into Lake Buena Vista between the Adventurers Club and the XZFR Rockin' Rollerdrome.

The Hollywood Studios Splash fountain was damaged in 2004 when Hurricane Charley broke off the mermaid but it was repaired and remained on display until its removal.

Here Come the Muppets
(1990 – 1991)

In the late 1980s, legendary puppeteer Jim Henson had tired of having so much of his time devoted to business matters. He was in final negotiations with The Walt Disney Company to sell the rights to his famous Muppet characters and become a creative consultant just before his untimely death.

It looked so much like a completed deal that Henson was already at work on a variety of projects for Disney including theme park attractions featuring the Muppets. In fact, there were plans for an entire new land to be called Muppet Studios with attractions, a restaurant, shops and more.

While work was still proceeding on the major Muppet*Vision 3-D attraction, to help introduce the characters into the park the fifteen minute stage show *Here Come the Muppets* was quickly opened in May 1990 in the theater in the Animation Courtyard that now houses The Voyage of the Little Mermaid.

To save time and money, the characters were portrayed by full-sized costumed performers with moving mouths rather than puppets except for two video inserts during the production.

The pre-show featured a video of the dog Rowlf playing the piano and being interrupted by Sam the Eagle.

Kermit is onstage and concerned because the other Muppets are late for the show. He receives a call on a videophone from Mickey Mouse who is checking in to see how things are going and Kermit lies that everything is fine. The scene with Mickey features the same set and animation as the Mickey scene in *The Muppets at Walt Disney World* television special from May 1990 but with different dialog.

Kermit calls the WDW picture phone operator who turns out to be actress Lily Tomlin doing her Ernestine character from *Laugh-In*. He asks to be connected with Miss Piggy who is relaxing in a robe with mud on her face. Informed that she is on a videophone, she instantly gets ready.

Kermit phones Fozzie Bear who claims to be lost but Kermit directs him to a green door behind him and it leads him to the stage.

Fozzie tells Kermit that Dr. Teeth and the Electric Mayhem band will be arriving soon by monorail and the front of a WDW monorail crashes through on stage right and the characters disembark. That same mechanism was later used for Ariel sitting on a rock in The Voyage of The Little Mermaid.

The show now starts with the Muppets performing the songs: *Make 'Em Laugh* (Kermit/Fozzie), *Personality* (Miss Piggy), *Bein' Green* (Kermit), *The Heart of Rock & Roll* and *Shout!*

The prerecorded voice track for the show uses all the main Muppeteers: Jim Henson, Frank Oz, Dave Goelz, Richard Hunt, Jerry Nelson and Steve Whitmire. That video insert footage of Fozzie and Miss Piggy was later reused in the PBS series Great Performances episode entitled *The World of Jim Henson* in 1994.

The standees of The Electric Mayhem that had been in the queue leading into the show resurfaced sometime in 2012 and were installed in the Stage 1 Company Store that sold Muppet merchandise.

Two weeks after the show closed on September 2, 1991, another show using full sized Muppet costumed characters premiered on a loading dock stage near the exit of Muppet*Vision 3-D entitled *Muppets on Location: Days of Swine and Roses*. The premise was that the Muppets were shooting a movie but take a break to interact with the audience by signing autographs and posing for photos. The show closed in 1994.

Osborne Spectacle of Dancing Lights
(1995 – 2015)

Sadly, Christmas 2015 was the last season for the Osborne Spectacle of Dancing Lights at Disney Hollywood Studios as the Streets of America were demolished for further expansion construction of the new Star Wars Land.

William Jennings Osborne, who preferred being called Jennings, was born in 1943. With his loving wife, Mitzi, they founded the Arkansas Research Medical Testing Center in Little Rock, Arkansas in 1968. With the success of the business, the couple bought a large estate in the middle of town.

In 1980, they had a daughter named Allison Brianne who went by the nickname Breezy from her middle name, even as she grew into adulthood. Her father, as might be imagined, was extremely busy with his business and so was not always around. When Breezy was six years old in 1986, he asked her what she wanted for Christmas expecting some type of popular toy on maybe even a pony.

Breezy replied that she wanted to spend time together with her often absent dad hanging lights on the outside of the house for the holidays. Jennings realized that he was missing the most important part of his life, spending time with his young daughter. That Christmas, Jennings extravagantly decorated the outside of the house with over a thousand Christmas lights to the joy of the entire family.

Every year after that, it became a tradition and Jennings kept adding more and more lights. However, Jennings home was located on one of the busiest streets in Little Rock and as the fame of this display spread, it resulted in severe traffic problems as visitors clogged the street to experience the illuminated spectacle.

When neighbors complained, Jennings bought the houses on either side of him and decorated them as well.

The display grew to millions of lights and in 1994 six neighbors filed a lawsuit with the county court that they won which Jennings appealed to the state Supreme Court and lost as well. Finally, Jennings appealed to the United States Supreme Court but that was denied and he was ordered to no longer operate the magnificent display.

"I do this to make people happy," Jennings told the *New York Times* newspaper in December 1994 to try to rally support. "It just makes me so sad that a few people could ruin something that so many enjoy. Every day is Christmas to me and I want to take everybody along."

Walt Disney World Executive Vice President Bruce Laval saw the report on CNN and assigned Show Director John Phelan to contact Jennings in the hopes of having an annual Christmas event to match the ones offered at the Magic Kingdom and Epcot.

Jennings and his family were huge Disney fans and an arrangement was made. Jennings never received any money for the use of his lights. His family would usually come down to Walt Disney World for about a week during the end of December and be put up at Disney's expense at the Grand Floridian to visit the parks. The family would come over one night to Disney MGM Studios where a special ceremony was held for Jennings and his daughter Breezy to turn on the lights that evening.

Jennings passed away from complications of heart surgery at the age of 67 in July 2011.

Even though Jennings was ordered to remove his massive light display on his home, he did continue to decorate the outside of his houses in a more modest fashion until his death. He and Breezy still hung some of the decorations themselves.

Secrets of Osborne
Spectacle of Dancing Lights
(1995 – 2015)

When the four 18-wheel Mayflower Moving Vans arrived at Walt Disney World on November 4,1995 and the lights were unloaded Show Director John Phelan discovered that there was a figure of a cat with an arched back outlined in purple. Time was of the essence since the display was announced as opening in just three weeks on November 24.

Phelan contacted Jennings Osborne to try to identify where it fit into the overall Christmas display and if it were perhaps a tribute to an Osborne pet. An amused Jennings replied that it was actually part of his Halloween lighting and he had shipped it by accident. Osborne had three huge backyard storage sheds filled with his holiday lights so it was easy to make a mistake.

Phelan kept the cat and had it re-lit in a holiday style and added to the display. Each year, the Walt Disney World lighting crew hid it somewhere different in the display without letting Phelan know its location, thus making him go and find it.

There is an homage to the University of Arkansas Razorbacks football team, with a red razorback hog hidden among the lights since Jennings was a huge Razorbacks fan including hosting free barbecues at Razorback games.

In 2006, approximately four hundred dimmer relay and control switches were added to the display allowing the lights to be choreographed to a musical score. The holiday event now consisted of more than five million lights and was officially renamed the Osborne Family Spectacle of *Dancing* Lights.

Disney was not the first to use dancing lights but its display was the largest. Disney continued to update and add more and more lights each year.

One year, special glasses were given away where the guests could see images of angels in the lights. Because of a little controversy regarding religious aspects, those glasses were redone the next year so guests could see snowflakes instead. The glasses also worked on guests' own Christmas tree at home.

The lights for display were all converted to energy-efficient LED lights beginning in 2011 making the lights not only environmentally friendly, less expensive in terms of electricity but also brighter. Scenes and music from the ABC holiday show *Prep & Landing* have also been added.

The infamous "leg lamp" from the popular movie *A Christmas Story* is in one of the windows. Glow With The Show Mickey ears were introduced in 2013. Santa Goofy was a part of the experience for several years.

Of course, there were dozens of hidden Mickeys as well from a toy soldier with mouse ears on his hat, to a marking spot on the rear end of a Dalmatian puppy to the more traditional three-circled images in a variety of colors. By the way, the Mickey Mouse driving a train was part of the original display in Arkansas.

The radio station WJBO that broadcasts music throughout the night is a tribute to William Jennings Bryan Osborne.

That red canopy of lights used to adorn the outdoor driveway of the Osborne home. The canopy was lower when it was on Residential Street because Osborne wanted people to feel immersed in the lights.

"I like creating memories that people won't soon forget," Jennings Osborne once said. "I want the people to feel like they are inside the lights, looking out at the world."

Disney's Hollywood Studios Parades

Everyone loves a parade but guests who visit the parks at Walt Disney World have been trained to expect one every day. While most people associate parades with the Magic Kingdom, every WDW park has had several parades over the years. Here are a few that were at Disney's Hollywood Studios:

Dinosaurs Live! Parade (September 26, 1991, to August 29, 1992). This was actually more of a mini-parade than a full-blown Disney parade with a short stage show in front of the Great Movie Ride. Earl Sinclair and his dinosaur family from the ABC sitcom *Dinosaurs* with puppetry from Jim Henson Company using animatronics developed by Brian Henson are the "surprise family of the day".

This parade could be considered more of a moving street party. It consisted of two floats, one with a camera crane carrying a "director" and one that was a large, two story float with the entire Sinclair family who are being filmed along with several female dancers attired in cave people jungle costumes and a marching band moving down Hollywood Boulevard after the show in front of the Chinese Theater.

The parade featured the then very popular Was (Not Was) song, *Walk the Dinosaur.*

Aladdin's Royal Caravan (December 21, 1992 – August 27, 1995). Inspired by a scene in the animated feature, the parade featured Prince Ali being presented to the people of Agrabah. The parade featured performers as harem dancers, lamp sellers, dancing female camels and more.

Genie made several appearances in the parade. First, he led a marching band at the beginning. Then, he popped up as a 32 foot tall inflatable figure over a float of treasure with dancers right behind twirling swords.

Next, just his upper body appeared on two poles held by parade performers. His pants would walk along (with another performer inside) and split from the upper body. Later, Genie's head would stick out of a treasure chest, out of a snake charmer's basket as well as bathing in a bathtub on the back of a camel.

Speaking of camels, the parade featured two huge golden camels who would turn their heads and spit water at the guests. These figures were so popular, they were later used elsewhere in the parks over the next few years including outside the Soundstage Restaurant and later at the Magic Carpets of Aladdin in the Magic Kingdom. In their new homes, they continued to spit to the delight of the guests.

At the finale, Aladdin attired as Prince Ali rode with Jasmine on a magic carpet on the back of the Abu in his elephant form. The head even turned in time with the music.

Following the elephant to close out the parade was a street sweeper....the villainous Jafar with his parrot Iago who was chattering away in the rolling wheeled refuse bucket.

This parade featured Disney's first use of lightweight inflatable costumes like for the acrobats. A version of this parade was also at Disneyland from April 1993 to June 1994.

Among other of the park parades were:

- Toy Story Parade (1995 - 1997)
- Hercules "Zero to Hero" Victory Parade (1997 - 1998)
- Mulan Parade (1998 - 2001)
- Disney's Stars & Motor Cars Parade (2001 - 2008)
- *The Hollywood Holly-Day Parade* performed during the Christmas holiday season 2004 -2007
- Block Party Bash (2008-2011)
- Pixar Pals Countdown to Fun! (2011 – 2013)
- Frozen Royal Welcome Ceremony (began summer 2014)

Disney's Animal Kingdom

Disney's Animal Kingdom opened April 22, 1998. While it is the newest of the WDW theme parks, being in existence just a little over two decades, things started to change almost immediately since there was no model to follow for this unique approach to a Disney theme park.

Originally, guests were not given guide maps so that they could discover things on their own but ended up getting frustrated and lost so that changed. The lack of signage changed as well.

While some things did fade away, more often the tweaking of the park was merely a change in names. The original Conservation Station was re-themed as Rafiki's Planet Watch with the inclusion of a costumed character who mediates in the area. Safari Village was renamed Discovery Island when the animal reserve island in Bay Lake closed in 2000.

Zebras were introduced to the Kilimanjaro Safari ride in 2012 and removed just four months later. Though Disney never released an official statement, it was rumored that the zebras were too aggressive, constantly biting each other, blocking paths, and even attacking ride vehicles.

The Rainforest Café, a themed restaurant chain operated by Landry's outside of the park's entrance, used to feature a massive waterfall that thundered down from the roof but as the horticulture grew and obscured the sight, the waterfall was shut down.

Something that quickly went extinct was that Disney did not allow plastic straws, lids, or balloons to be used at DAK, unlike the rest of the Disney parks. This is so that plastic does not inadvertently enter an animal's habitat and hurt them. Instead, the park uses biodegradable paper straws and offers lids for hot drinks only.

It is not unusual for a dinosaur to go extinct. Lucky the dinosaur was the prototype for the next generation of audio-animatronics figures. In fact, the 20-feet long, roughly 12-feet tall, the 450-pound Lucky, who smiles, grunts, sneezes, bats his eyelashes and signs clover-shaped autographs, had very successful test runs at Disney's California Adventure and later Disney's Animal Kingdom.

Lucky is patterned after the Gallimimus dinosaur, but Disney designers took some liberties to soften his image so children of all ages would fall in love with him. He did vocalizations including hiccups.

Lucky was five years in development. Unlike earlier animatronics figures, Lucky is operated by electric motors and sensors that are controlled through a central computer, which regulates everything from Lucky's ponderous footsteps to the gentle batting of his eyelashes. The batteries and computer were located in the flower cart that he pulled.

The type of skin generally used for other animatronics characters could not be used for Lucky because it was too heavy so Imagineers developed a lighter, more flexible skin.

Lucky was also meant to publicize the four hour television mini-series *Dinotopia* (2002) which is why Lucky's "handler" who walked along his side was attired in garb appropriate for that show.

Lucky's first appearance was at The Natural History Museum of Los Angeles on August 28, 2003. A few days later he visited Disney California Adventure.

He eventually made appearances in Disney's Animal Kingdom starting in 2005. Today, he's back home at Walt Disney Imagineering and makes occasional appearances for Adventures by Disney guests, the D23 2009 Expo and non-Disney events like the 2008 World Science Festival.

Nahtazu

(2002 -2006)

To get the general public to understand that Disney's Animal Kingdom was not like the typical zoo but a new type of theme park, in 2002 WDW through its Yellow Shoes Creative Marketing division had Mark Simon storyboard a thirty-second commercial spot.

The final commercial was produced by Jim Derusha of Alpha Wolf Productions and consisted of various DAK cast members declaring "Nahtazu", a fictional word that when pronounced sounded like "not a zoo".

The commercial ended with the tag line: "Disney's Animal Kingdom. It's many, many things but remember...it's Nahtazu!"

Disney stopped using the term in 2006 as it strengthened its connections with the AZA (Association of Zoos and Aquariums).

The idea of it not being a zoo came from Imagineer Joe Rohde, executive designer and senior vice president, Creative for Walt Disney Imagineering. In a presentation to DAK cast members on June 14, 1998, he stated:

> Disney sent a group of MBAs out across the country visiting and researching zoos around the nation and they came back with a terrifically negative report that basically said, "Look. There's a zoo in *every* city, in *every* town in this country. They're *all* subsidized by the city, by the state, by the federal government. People pay a *third* of what they pay to get into our parks to come in...they stay for *two* hours...they buy a *drink*...they can go whenever they want...*why* would we ever do a *zoo*?" End of question, right?

> We the Disney Company simply *cannot* do what is out there to be done if for *no other* reason than we're gonna charge you $50 or more to do it. So it *has* to be different, it *has* to be new, it *has* to be unlike anything else you can do or we simply cannot pursue it as a line of business because we can't make our per cap.

There's *still* people in the company who will refer to this as a 'zoo' and I mean, by no means, any disrespect or disdain to what a zoo *is*. It *is* a thing that exists in the world and is loved and valued, obviously, by their presence around the country and the world, by *gazillions* of people.

It serves a purpose, it occupies a niche and it does it really rather well. *That's* the point. That job's *done*. The world doesn't need another big, expensive zoo with a bunch of immersion exhibits in it. That is *not* a real pressing need on the planet.

A zoo sits in a category of places within a community that is sort of comparable to the museum, to the library, in that it's regarded with a kind of respectful awe. There's always a secondary use of a zoo as a garden, as a place to just go stroll with kids in the sunlight when the weather is good. There's clearly a recognition that this is a place of edification.

Now, on the other hand, what we are trying to do is *profoundly* subjective, even in ways that I think many education professionals would consider to be almost dangerous. A theme park is *all* about *you* in a very specific context. *Nothing* happens to you… *nothing* is said to you…nothing is *seen* by you…that isn't governed by the overarching narrative umbrella that holds you in that place. When you move through a space, the space is *crafted* to specific narrative impact on you. That's what Disney's Animal Kingdom is. It is not a zoo.

Discovery River Boats

(1998 -1999)

Discovery River Boats was an opening day attraction at Disney's Animal Kingdom April 1998 but closed just over a year later in August 1999, making it the first DAK attraction to close.

It was intended to be a much more ambitious experience with previews of the upcoming Beastly Kingdom along the route including encounters with a unicorn, a kraken that would attack the boat and the head of a fire-breathing dragon.

Remnants from that concept that were seen on the final version included a statue of a twelve foot tall white unicorn rearing up on its two rear legs and the infamous Dragon Rocks, a structure of rocks that looked vaguely like a dragon streaming water out of its mouth. Located a little further north of the Camp Minnie-Mickey bridge was a large area of volcanic rocks on the left bank of the river that looked like a cave entrance.

As the boat approached, smoke billowed from the cave, thunderous roars were heard, and massive flames shot out from inside the cave suggesting it was the lair of a dragon. Sensors along the bank would be triggered by the boat to enable the show effects.

Budget cuts resulted in the ride becoming more of just a one-way transportation system between the dock from Safari Village near Dinoland U.S.A. and the Upcountry Landings dock in Asia.

Guests expected it would be something more like the Jungle Cruise since the boats looked similar in design and long boarding lines originally resulted because of the misunderstanding.

There were seven boats that were named Manatee Maiden, Leaping Lizard, Scarlet Flamingo, Otter Nonsense, Hasty Hippo, Crocodile Belle, and Darting Dragonfly.

Jack Plettinck was in charge of taking the shiny new boats from a manufacturer in Seattle and making them seem well-worn. It had to seem that they had survived dings and dents from moorings, docks, submerged logs and angry animals. He even applied acrylic rust.

Guests did see a few things on the voyage around the Tree of Life including a series of hot springs geysers along the shores of Africa, animal water sculptures at the Discovery Lagoon, and a large audio-animatronics Iguanodon playing in the water near DinoLand U.S.A. that foreshadowed the Countodwn to Extinction attraction where that dinosaur plays a key role in the story.

The Iguanodon animatronic was later stripped of its skin and sent to Walt Disney Studios Park at Disneyland Paris as a prop in the boneyard of the Studio Tram Tour. The unicorn statue was sold to a private collector.

The attraction was renamed November 1998 to the Discovery River Taxi to emphasize it was just transportation and had prerecorded narration. Animal handlers with small animals were added on the boat as part of the park's animal education initiative but did not prove to be a guest satisfier.

In March 1999, the attraction was once again renamed and was called Radio Disney River Cruise playing commentary from Radio Disney disc jockeys Just Plain Mark and Zippy with music that the guests were told was being broadcast from the top of the Tree of Life. It wasn't.

When the attraction finally closed, the boats were stored in a backstage marina and the docks used occasionally for character meet and greet opportunities or additional seating. Two of the boats were later relocated to Magic Kingdom's Contemporary Resort where they were repurposed for a Pirates & Pals fireworks voyage on Bay Lake and the Seven Seas Lagoon.

Prehistoric McDonalds

(1998 – 2007)

Starting January 1997, McDonalds entered into a ten year agreement with the Disney Company for promotions of Disney films, videos, TV properties and theme parks. It ended January 2007.

Disney allowed McDonald's to open six food locations in the four Disney parks as well as actual fast food restaurants at Downtown Disney and another near Disney's All-Star Resorts.

As part of the arrangement, McDonald's agreed to sponsor the entire Dinoland section of Disney's Animal Kingdom theme park. Everything from the Dino Institute with the Countdown to Extinction attraction to the Boneyard to Restaurantosaurus were branded by McDonalds.

Even today in the Dinosaur attraction are three utility pipes colored red, white and yellow and each labeled with the appropriate chemical formulas for ketchup, mayonnaise and mustard.

In fact, Restaurantosaurus offered a fuller McDonald's menu than at other park locations but renamed the familiar food items as Dino-Sized Double Cheeseburger and Hot Dog-osaurus. In the Happy Meals, the toys were T-Rex, Stegosaurus, Pterodactyl, and Triceratops water pistols.

The Restaurantosaurus back story is that it was a student commissary in a building that also served as a dormitory and classroom.

During McDonald's tenure in the area, there were two posters illustrated by famed dinosaur artist William Stout. One featured a T-Rex gobbling down a smaller dinosaur and the slogan "Have you had a Crocodilian today?" to parody McDonald's slogan of "Have you had a break today?"

The second illustration was a mock movie poster for a dinosaur on the loose in modern times film entitled *It Came Through the Drive-Thru*. The McDonalds' punny name references included: "Starring Hap. P. Meal, Hanover D. Fries, and I. C. McNuggets. Produced by Gordon Arches and Presented by Prehistoric Pictures."

To promote the park nationally, McDonalds Disney's Animal Kindom Happy Meal featured twelve animal toys. There was a Triceratops, Toucan, Gorilla (with her baby), Elephant, Lemur, Dragon (that flapped its wings), Iguanodon, Zebra, Lion, Cheetah, Crocodile, Tortoise and Rhino. They all had different actions including the Gorilla spinning her baby, the Zebra being a wind-up toy and the Tortoise sticking his head in and out of his shell.

The purple, fire-breathing dragon intended for the never built Beastly Kingdom was not just a toy but appeared on Happy Meal boxes and on beverage cups since it was to be the icon of that land of animals that never were.

For Japan and other countries, McDonald's released a set of four Happy Meals figures not available in the United States: Minnie Mouse with a baby gorilla from Gorilla Falls Exploration Trail, Mickey Mouse in a Kilimanjaro Safari jeep, Goofy digging for fossils with an Iguanodon and Donald Duck in a Discovery River Boat.

While Disney netted more than $100 million dollars in royalties during the decade long agreement, McDonald's netted more than one billion dollars even promoting Disney's box office bombs like *Dinosaur* (2000), *Atlantis: The Lost Empire* (2001), *Treasure Planet* (2002), and *Home on the Range* (2004).

McDonald's promotion for a film might exceed Disney's budget for advertising so in addition to the royalty money, Disney got additional visibility for its films. However, the agreement prevented McDonald's from promoting non-Disney films in its franchises and that helped sour the relationship as well as the poor box office for the animated films.

Countdown to Extinction

(1998 – 2000)

When CEO Michael Eisner had to make the decision whether to build Beastly Kingdom or DinoLand U.S.A. at Disney's Animal Kingdom, several things influenced his decision besides his interest in dinosaurs.

In production for a release in 2000 was the Disney feature film entitled *Dinosaur* that combined live action backgrounds (mostly filmed in Venezuela) with CGI dinosaurs to create a "photo-realistic" appearance. The film would prominently feature an Iguanodon and a Carnotaurus.

The Imagineers pitched a thrill ride that would also prominently feature those two dinosaurs so it would tie in with promoting the film and utilize the EMV (Enchanced Motor Vehicle) ride system developed for Disneyland's Indiana Jones Adventure attraction and a nearly identical track layout so it would save construction money as the park was going way over budget.

The backstory was that the Dino Institute was struggling for funds so hired Dr. Helen Marsh who had a reputation for fund-raising for museums. Within days of her arrival, she purchased Chrono-Teck Inc. and announced they had developed a CTX (to reference Countdown to Extinction attraction name) Time Rover vehicle that could travel back in time.

This invention brought the Institute prestige and funding to build a state-of-the-art facility to assist in research and house classrooms. The "new" version of the Dino Institute was dedicated on April 22, 1978 (to reference the opening of DAK on the same date in 1998).

Dr. Marsh insisted that tours to the Cretaceous period be offered to non-professionals to help subsidize the costs of the new facility. Controller Dr. Grant Seeker informs the visitors that he intends to use the time rover to save an Iguanodon from extinction and bring it back to the Dino Institute.

Once aboard the Time Rover, riders begin a turbulent journey back to a prehistoric jungle where they encounter several dinosaurs including a Styracosaurus, Alioramus, Raptor, Sauropod, and Pterodactyls among others and are chased by a Carnotaurus before finally rescuing an Iguanodon seconds before an asteroid hits.

Disney expected the movie *Dinosaur* to become another timeless classic and attract families with younger children so significant changes were made to the attraction. Two weeks before the movie was released, the attraction was renamed Dinosaur.

Outside of the Dino Institute, the Styracosaurus standing in an infinity pool was replaced with an Iguanodon in a garden and footage from the film was inserted into the pre-show.

The first time warp tunnel (where the Time Rover is "sent back into the past") no longer used the lasers and pyro effects to blind guests. The Compsognathus that jumped over the Time Rover were on a chain and pulley system and were deactivated so they just hovered in place (and were later replaced by projections in 2016).

The ending was changed with a large, static, blacklight, cartoon-proportioned Carnotaurus head sliding toward guests on a visible rolling rig. Changes were made in the narration to make it more comedic and emphazing more urgency.

The motion of the EMVs were reduced and made less jarring so the height requirement could be lowered for younger children. The audio of the chase by the Carnotaurus was softened so instead of getting ever closer, it faded off as if the dinosaur had fallen behind the vehicle.

These changes did not make the attraction less scary for children but did make it more disappointing for adults. As a result the original version despite some similarities to the current version is considered an entirely different ride experience.

Fossil Preparation Lab

(1998 – 1999)

Dino-Sue was named after paleontologist Sue Hendrickson who found a remarkable skeleton in 1990 at the Cheyenne River Indian Reservation in western South Dakota. Never before had such a complete Tyrannosaurus Rex skeleton been unearthed with about 90 percent of the 350 bones intact.

The original Sue lived during the Late Cretaceous Period, in the Mesozoic Era. She weighed several tons, and her skeleton is a whopping 40 feet long, and 13 feet tall making her the largest Tyrannosaurus Rex skeleton ever discovered as well.

In October 1997, The Chicago Field Museum paid a record $8.4 million for the prehistoric treasure at auction, helped by donations from Walt Disney World, McDonald's and the California State University system.

Rushing to finish the skeleton for a big Millennium exhibit, the Chicago Field Museum had seven people working full time on the bones, including as part of the deal for Disney's and McDonald's contributions having three scientists headed by paleontologist Bruce Schumacher who worked on it in the Fossil Preparation Lab in DinoLand.

Millions of visitors observed the preparation of Sue's bones through glass windows in both labs. The DAK team (like one in Chicago at the Field Museum) carefully removed the South Dakota rock in which the bones were fossilized 67 million years ago, doing the work behind glass in a public viewing area in the temporary structure.

Every day, a paleontologist worked cleaning, cataloguing and photographing a genuine fossilized dinosaur bone, while a couple of cameras with monitors showed a close up view of the work being undertaken.

Schumacher said:

> People sometimes have a hard time realizing that these are real
> bones. We try to go out and talk to people at different times
> during the day, and sometimes we find that they think we're just
> actors pretending to work, on a set made to look like a science lab
> because it is at Disney.

Guests could watch through the glass windows, read colorful
displays, and ask questions of a Disney attendant stationed outside. In addition, the lab had the sounds of a dinosaur roaring
piped in periodically over the loud speaker. The paleontologists
heard it hundreds of a time a day and would joke that it sounded
more like a big toilet flushing than a dinosaur.

Once cleaned, fragments of the bones were glued together. Any
cracks in the bones were filled with industrial-strength Krazy
Glue to hold them together and prevent more crumbling. Gaps or
missing bones were molded from clay.

In addition, they made molds of the bones so that three replicas could be created. In 1999, the bones were loaded into crates
and shipped back to Chicago by a special moving company that
used air-conditioned, climate-controlled trucks, the kind used to
move fine art. Security guards accompanied the bones. The Fossil
Preparation Lab was closed.

Two of the replicas went on a national tour sponsored by
McDonald's, visiting over 18 U.S. cities beginning in July 2000.
The third replica now stands outdoors in DinoLand U.S.A. near
the entrance to the Dinosaur attraction.

Bob Lamb, Animal Kingdom's vice president at the time, said:

> This is a chance to have the real thing in DinoLand. I don't see us
> doing a huge promotion about us working on this dinosaur. Sue
> will become one of the things you discover in the park.

By the way, the 90-foot Brachiosaurus skeleton that stretches
over Dinoland's entrance was cast from the mold of the same
skeleton that arches over Stanley Field Hall in the Field Museum.

Dinosaur Jubilee
(1998 – 2000)

DinoLand U.S.A. was supposed to feature a roller coaster similar to Big Thunder Mountain called The Excavator referencing a left over piece of equipment in a sand and gravel pit.

The Excavator was meant to look like a series of ore cars used to haul up the sand and gravel from the bottom of the pit to dump trucks. The paleontology students who were working in the area had reconfigured the unsafe device that had fallen into disrepair to transport the dinosaur fossils they were finding.

The marketing publicity described it as "a rollicking coaster ride through a section of the dig supposedly too dangerous to enter". At one point, the ride would have zoomed through the inside of a dinosaur skeleton.

It appeared clearly on the original concept painting of the area. It was felt that the Countdown to Extinction (now Dinosaur) attraction since it re-used existing technology would be easier and less expensive to build, yet still attract guests wanting a thrill ride.

Dinosaur Jubilee was a quickly produced and relatively inexpensive addition to provide an additional experience for guests that was substituted in the location for the proposed the roller coaster. It looked temporary and sparse but it was also one of the few attractions at DAK that had air conditioning. It disappeared in early spring 2001 to be replaced by Chester and Hester's Dino-rama.

The guide map stated, "Meander through dino artifacts – see casts of spectacular real dinosaur skeletons!"

It was located in a large white plastic tent around the corner from the Cretaceous Trail, opposite of Chester and Hester's shop. It was a museum-like exhibit of fossils and skeleton casts that supposedly represented some of the fictitious Dino Institute's findings in the area.

The displays featuring casts supplied by the Black Hills Institute and Triebold Paleontolgoy included among other prehistoric animals one of the most complete Tyrannosaurs Rex skeletons in existence at the time, two Triceratops, a Edmontosaurus, a Pachycephalosaurus, two Tylosaurus with a Pterandon in one of its jaws, and an Archelon.

There was even an elaborate area devoted to the Ice Age. The full skeletons were positioned in poses similiar to what might be found at a Natural History museum, and there were ferns and other plants from the era mixed in with the models.

In 2000, the name of the attraction changed to Dinosaur Jubilee 2000 in honor of the Milleunium. The exhibit added some interactive versions of an audio-animatronics mammoth and a sabre tooth tiger. These creatures were not skeletons but covered with fur.

As a precursor to the forthcoming Chester & Hester's Dino-Rama a series of simple carnival style games were setup outside of the Dinosaur Jubilee area.

A giant, rather tacky looking, purple inflatable T-Rex as well a banner at the entrance to Dinoland were put in place to direct more guests to the Jubilee. The background story to explain these new additions was that the Dino Institute grad students were putting on a carnival in order to raise money.

In December 2000, the exhibit was themed to Christmas with a huge Santa hat on the T-Rex skeleton and large candy canes in the Ice Age section.

Dinosaur Jubilee and the Fossil Preparation Lab that also disappeared are still featured on a hand-drawn map of DinoLand featured on one of the bulletin boards in the area. The Triceratops head from the exhibit ended up at the Wilderness Explorers.

Camp Minnie-Mickey
(1998 -2014)

Although Camp Minnie-Mickey was meant to be a temporary placeholder, it lasted almost 16 years from 1998 to 2014 when it was replaced by Pandora: The World of Avatar.

Disney's Animal Kingdom faced unexpected budget overruns so cuts had to be made including an entire land called Beastly Kingdom. Realizing there would be not enough shows and attractions on opening day, CEO Michael Eisner recalled Mickey's Birthdayland, a temporary location built in only ninety days in 1988 for the Magic Kingdom. Eisner felt that something similar devoted to Disney characters would mimic that success.

The DAK design team was appalled that the Beastly Kingdom had been cut and told Eisner they were too busy with the other areas of the park to work on the placeholder so Entertainment and some outside developers took over the assignment. There was no time or money to build attractions, so they concentrated on shows and meet-and-greet opportunities.

It was hoped once the new park was a success that there would be an influx of revenue to build Beastly Kingdom. That didn't happen.

Camp Minnie-Mickey was themed to be a rural five acre summer fishing camp in the woodlands of the Adirondack Mountains in upstate New York where the characters were on vacation. This theme was echoed in the landscape, architecture, and street furniture that provided a homemade feeling.

At the Greeting Trails guests could usually find Mickey, Minnie, Donald and Goofy. In random places throughout the land other characters like Chip, Dale, Koda, Pocahontas, Meeko, Baloo, King Louie among others appeared.

Along the river were three-dimensional fiberglass figures of Donald Duck fishing and catching a rubber boot; Mickey, Pluto and Goofy fishing; and Huey, Dewey, and Louie hiking with Daisy Duck.

The camp's assembly hall seating 1,375 guests was the home for the half hour *The Festival of the Lion King* musicial show that did not tell an abbreviated version of the famous animated feature's plot but was a tune-filled tribal celebration with audience participation and some unexpected surprises.

Hosted by four human performers with Swahili names and attired as traditional African tribal leaders, they prompted the guests on how to participate with the performers several times during the show.

The impressive floats that served as intriguing set pieces were actually recycled and modified from *The Lion King Celebration* parade that ran at Disneyland from 1994-1997 to save on costs.

The other show was the twelve-minute *Pocahontas and Her Forest Friends* in Grandma Willow's Grove. The genesis of the show came from the animal education cast at Disney's Animal Kingdom. It was meant to be similar to the animal meet-and-greet shows at zoos and other animal parks, where a trainer or two brings out one animal at a time and talks about the animal's characteristics to the audience.

Pocahontas is worried that the forest is being cut down indiscriminately and runs to Grandma Willow for advice. She reminds Pocahontas of a prophecy that one creature has a special gift to protect the forest but that Pocahontas herself must discover the identity of that creature giving her the opportunity to interact with several different animals including a raccoon, a snake, rabbits, opossums, a skunk, a porcupine and in the process educate the audience about them.

While there was no restaurant in the land, guests could get cookies and ice cream sandwiches at Camp Soft Serve (also known as Chip and Dale's Cookie Cabin) and funnel cakes, corn dogs and beverages at Campfire Treats (also known as Forest Trail Funnel Cakes) .

Pocahontas and Her Forest Friends
(1998 – 2008)

Pocahontas and Her Forest Friends was a twelve minute show that opened April 22, 1998 and closed September 27, 2008. It was performed in the three hundred and fifty seat Grandma Willow's Grove Theater in the Camp Minnie-Mickey area of Disney's Animal Kingdom.

The show was inspired by the 1995 Disney animated feature film *Pocahontas*. The live action show was rushed into production so quickly that Disney at first listed it as "Meet the Characters" rather than a stage show in the park guide.

The show was originally called *Colors of the Wind, Friends from the Animal Forest* but that was an awkward title that didn't mention Pocahontas. In fact, early guests just called it the "Pocahontas Show" so Disney eventually changed the title.

The genesis of the show came from the animal education cast at Disney's Animal Kingdom. It was meant to be similar to the animal meet-and-greet shows at zoos and other animal parks where a trainer or two brings out one animal at a time and talks about the animal's characteristics to the audience.

However, Disney is a storytelling company and decided to provide an upgraded experience even though the show was intended to be just a placeholder to run for two years or so until Beastly Kingdom was built in the same location. The script was written by Michael Korkis, Bob Glickman and David Duffy and originally directed by Korkis.

The show was written to utilize the natural behaviors of the animals. The animals sometimes decided they didn't want to appear which is why so many different types of animals rotated throughout the years in the show.

A live character performer portrayed Pocahontas and there were two puppeteers who were underneath the stage for Sprig and

Grandmother Willow. The puppeteers sat on two reclining seats under the stage and pulled themselves by rope to and from the appropriate location. Grandma Willow came from the Disneyland *Spirit of Pocahontas* show that closed in September 1997.

Pocahontas is worried that the forest is being cut down indiscriminately and runs to Grandma Willow for advice. She reminds Pocahontas of a prophecy that one creature has a special gift to protect the forest but that Pocahontas herself must discover the identity of that creature.

One at a time, several different animals wander onto the stage including at different shows a raccoon, a snake, rabbits, opossums, a skunk, a porcupine, rats and a turkey. Prior to each day's performances, the animals were stored in separate wire cages behind the stage.

As each animal appeared on stage, Pocahontas talked about what people can learn from each creature. "Every animal has knowledge to share with those who are willing to learn."

Finally, Pocahontas realizes that the creature of the prophecy must be human beings. "Humans can destroy the forest, but we can also save it. The Earth is our home too. If we take care of it, it will take care of us!"

Since the show was designed for a young demographic with special seating for them in the first four rows of the theater, the message had to be simple and clear. The show proved so popular that eventually DAK occasionally offered Pocahontas and Her Forest Friends Animal Training Show where the animal handlers demonstrated how they trained the animals for the show.

Flights of Wonder
(1998 - 2017)

The Flights of Wonder show evolved from a strictly educational presentation to a show with the comedy relief of a clueless tour guide character named "Guano Joe" who is more than a little fearful of these avian performers. Along with the audience, he learns about them and learns to love them.

Under the canvas canopy of a shady sanctuary that is what remains of the Maharajah's crumbling fortress is the makeshift Caravan Stage in the "ruins" that are now the refuge for a dazzling array of birds. From opening until 2015, the Caravan Stage was covered with a canopy. A permanent roof was finally installed during a renovation in early 2016.

The façade of the roughly thousand person amphitheater was designed to resemble the architecture of that found in the Himalayan highlands or Rajasthan, India. The theater is situated outside the fictitious village of Anandapur, on the "trade route" towards Africa.

Approximately twenty species of exotic birds performed. While the show was entertaining, its core was a much deeper message about serious conservation themes and habitat loss. It promoted the World Wildlife Conservation Fund.

Among the species that most guests saw included Barbary falcons, macaws, Amazon parrots, Harris Hawks, ibis, vultures, crowned cranes, a Trumpeter Hornbill, Great Horned Owl, Black Vulture, an American Bald Eagle and several other interesting birds. The birds were from various continents and not just Asia. While the specific birds may occasionally be different in each show, the format of the show remained the same.

The host is an actual trainer who has spent hours with these birds. The birds are trained to react and take different actions based on audio and visual cues they have been taught. Certain noises, words or a subtle hand placement will spark an action from the birds.

While the show had been carefully rehearsed to demonstrate how birds hunt and eat, they had not been trained to do the typical tricks usually seen in such shows but merely duplicate natural behaviors with an emphasis on entertainment value like grabbing a dollar bill an audience member holds high in the air.

Groucho, the singing parrot in the show who was an audience favorite was named the World's Best Singing Parrot on the *Tonight Show with Jay Leno* after an appearance. He's also appeared on other television shows including *The Ellen DeGeneres Show*.

He was fairly unusual for most parrots because he was able to sing seven full songs including *How Much is that Doggy in the Window?*, *Camptown Races*, *Yankee Doodle Dandy*, *Alouetta* and *Jingle Bells*.

Hatched in 1986 in Kalamazoo, Michigan and raised by Theresa Barylock, Groucho was a yellow-naped Amazon parrot with an amazing ability to articulate many words and phrases such as "Look ma! No hands!"

At the end of 2017, the show closed to be replaced on DAK's 20th anniversary in April 2018 by a new 25-minute bird show, UP! A Great Bird Adventure.

The new show features Senior Wilderness Explorer Russell and his furry friend Dug from the Disney-Pixar animated film *Up* (2009) who have journeyed to Asia and met up with Anika, a bird enthusiast, to learn more about birds from around the world like their often-mentioned friend from the film Kevin.

The new show, like its predecessor, features bird experts and close-up encounters with numerous bird species. The show now includes more than fifteen species, including toucans, parrots, macaws, an African fish eagle, and a bald eagle.

Theater in the Wild Shows

Imagineer Alex Wright said, "Theater in the Wild is not really part of the lands of Animal Kingdom. Even its name is intended to reflect the idea that it's an entity unto itself. It offers a performance space that can be used for shows that might not fit very well into any of the established storylines."

The 1,500 seat Theater in the Wild in the Dinoland USA area has featured three stage shows: *Journey into the Jungle Book* (1998-1999), *Tarzan Rocks!* (1999-2006), and *Finding Nemo - The Musical* (2007-Present).

Journey Into the Jungle Book was a roughly twenty-five minute show that condensed the story of Mowgli and his animal encounters in the jungles of India from Disney's animated feature film *The Jungle Book* (1967) featuring the popular songs including *Bare Necessities* and *I Wanna Be Like You.*

It featured some costumed characters, human performers and innovative puppetry. During cast previews, the masks for characters had not been finished so audiences could see the performers' faces and loved it.

Later, when the show debuted and the masks had arrived, it seemed to lose its connection with the audience. Some of the costumes looked like bushes and trees that when positioned differently became animals.

Show Director Fran Soeder said, "I am best known as the man who brought puppetry to Walt Disney World. Over my decade in residence as a Show Director, I created *The Legend of the Lion King, The Hunchback of* Notre Dame, *Journey Into Jungle Book* and *The Voyage of The Little Mermaid.*

"Most of our Puppeteers were untrained but in less than five years, I created one of the largest groups of professional puppeteers in the country. Over those years there were successful collaborations with puppet designer Chuck Fawcet (ANIMAX) as well as Structural Engineer, Michael Curry (Michael Curry Design) as well as a team of New York designers which included Scenic Designer James Leonard Joy and Lighting Designer Natasha Katz."

After a year, the show was replaced with the high-energy half-hour *Tarzan Rocks* (1999) directed by Reed Jones which didn't retell the story of the animated feature but was more of a rock concert experience revue that focused on the relationship between Tarzan and Jane.

The "Two Worlds Concert Tour" was to help promote the release that same year of the animated feature. At one point, Imagineers pitched the idea of an inverted roller coaster that would have guests mimic swinging on vines like Tarzan through the jungle but it was eventually determined to be cost prohibitive and take too long to build. A live show could be put together quickly to leverage the release of the film.

The show included gymnasts, singers, dancers, aerialists, roller-blading monkeys who went into the audience like in the play *Starlight Express* in addition to a scene where Tarzan and Jane swirled on rope vines in an aerial ballet dance high above the stage like Cirque de Soleil. During the run of the show there was a pin and a medallion coin available for sale.

The songs performed by a live band were all from the film and included "You'll Be in My Heart," "Son of Man," "Trashin' the Camp" (with Terk and a dancing back-up group), and "Two Worlds."

The show ended when a musical show devoted to the animated feature film debuted on Broadway in 2006 and the theater itself was slated for construction work so that it could be enclosed.

DAK Parades

DAK was never designed to have a parade for fear it might disturb the animals or take away from the premise of DAK being a different kind of experience.

The March of the ARTimals Parade (1998-1999). The Disney publicity release described it as: "It's not a parade...it's not a procession...so what is it? Join us and find out as we present our fun, zany and fanciful one-of-a-kind 'moving celebration' of imagination and living art inspired by the world of animals".

It was different than other Disney theme park parades and was more of a carnival/Mardi Gras approach meant to represent a bunch of artists getting together to create their impressions of animals out of "found" items. The parade was designed to maneuver around the narrow pathways yet still stand out from the surrounding lush landscaping.

Designed by Swiss artist Rolf Knie, the parade was supposed to represent an informal and intimate celebration and featured no Disney characters or Disney music. Some of the costumes even showed the faces of the "artists" who were sculptors, weavers and painters.

Originally entitled March of the Animals, the avant-garde approach initially confused the guests so the name was changed to emphasize that is was an artistic interpretation. A band and storyteller were added to accompany the parade performers. Later, the costumes were used for entertainment and photo opportunities in the Safari Village area.

The instrumental music included songs with animal references like "Let's All Sing Like the Birdies Sing," "Flight of the Bumblebee," "Baby Elephant Walk," "Tiger Rag," "Itsy Bitsy Spider," and "Aba Daba Honeymoon."

The six unusual floats included a lion playing a xylophone made from wooden gazelle skeletons, a frog wearing a straw hat and red-and-white striped jacket crooning to some dancing frogs, and a queen bee sitting on her honey throne while others bees tickled her with a flower and swirling ribbons.

The fifteen minute parade started near Pizzafari and wound its way through Asia and past Dinoland USA but with viewing available only on one side of the route because the path was so narrow.

Mickey's Jungle Jammin' Parade (2001- 2014). The premise for the parade was that the Disney characters were on a jungle safari expedition (in a number of themed character jeeps and trucks) to provide a tribute to their animal friends in abstract images and figures as part of the 100 Years of Magic Celebration. In addition there were stilt walkers, dancers and animal puppets.

The official publicity blurb stated: "an interactive street party that features the Disney characters on expedition with a tribute to their animal friends. Mickey and the gang have packed up a caravan of crazy, colorful safari vehicles to blaze some trails through this wildly imaginative world. Adding to the rhythm of the ride is a herd of giant rolling drums cleverly disguised as exotic animals."

The distinctive parade costumes were designed by Matt Davidson. The prototypes for the puppeteer costumes were crafted in Africa by native artisans.

Parade costumes were created at Walt Disney World Creative Costuming, Parsons Mears in New York, Costume Armor in New York and Vegas Costumes in Las Vegas. Starting in 2004, it had an annual holiday overlay for the Christmas season making it temporarily Mickey's Jingle Jungle Parade.

The Volo Auto Museum in Volo, Illinois acquired three Disney parade cars, including Goofy and Minnie's vehicles from the Jammin' Jungle Parade in early 2019. They were later used in a "parade" around the grounds starting in the summer of 2019.

Beyond the Parks

While most people only think of the theme parks when they think of Walt Disney World, WDW has always been a much larger vacation destination with resort hotels, water parks, shopping districts and more.

Of course, the WDW resort hotels are constantly having things go extinct as they update their accommodations like the removal of artist Paul Hartley's very impressionistic "cartoony" map of WDW property that hung in the rooms of the Contemporary and the Polynesian resorts starting in 1971.

In fact, the resort rooms are continually undergoing color and décor changes every seven to ten years, sometimes even being completely gutted down to the basic structure.

Every part of the original Polynesian Village Resort has been replaced and updated over the years. In 1999, ten of the eleven longhouses were renamed to reflect Polynesian islands.

The original pool at the resort in 1971 was the Nanea Volcano Pool, where guests had to go under a waterfall to get to the stairs to get to the top of the water slide. That pool was replaced in March 2001 with the current pool featuring a larger volcano. In 1978, another pool was added and was known to Disney fans as the "quiet pool" because it was less popular with noisy children. It had originally been a putting green. In 2011 that pool was drained and the deep end filled before it reopened in May 2011.

Over the years the original restaurants and shops were redone and renamed. The Papeete Bay Verandah was themed as a French Colonial restaurant open for breakfast, lunch and dinner with a nightly live Polynesian Revue, but that location became 'Ohana in 1995. The South Seas Dining Room that featured a Polynesian buffet completely disappeared.

Vice President of Park Operations Dick Nunis came up with the idea to add surfing as a recreational activity for guests. At a cost of nearly a half-million dollars, a wave machine was installed in the Seven Seas Lagoon in 1971 but problems cropped up immediately and it was shut down by 1973.

The Caribbean Beach Resort redid its room in Trinidad as pirate themed a few years ago and finally eliminated its isolated check-in building so that now guests can now use the central Old Port Royale.

Since the Disney animated feature *The Princess and the Frog* took place in New Orleans, it seemed natural that the rooms at Port Orleans Riverside would be transformed into Royal Guest Rooms with elements from Princess Tiana's royal friends like bathroom faucets in the shape of the genie's lamp or the luggage bench in the shape of the dog from *Beauty and the Beast* who was transformed into a bench. Of course, Port Orleans Riverside was originally called Dixie Landings until 2001.

Do you remember Pal Mickey which was an interactive plush Mickey Mouse doll that would use sensors planted throughout WDW to provide tips, play games and tell jokes? It premiered in April of 2003 with an updated version made available in May 2005. It was sold through 2008 and continued to work until 2014 when Disney concentrated on its new Magic Bands and the technology necessary to make them function.

In WDW restrooms, there were dispensers of powdered soap that would dissolve when hands were washed. Those dispensers were replaced by liquid soap dispensers after the Anthrax scare in 2001.

Here are a few of the major things that went extinct beyond the parks.

Walt Disney World Speedway

(1995 – 2015)

The Walt Disney World Speedway was built in 1995 by IMS Events Inc., a subsidiary of the Indianapolis Motor Speedway Corporation and was located in front of the parking lot for the Magic Kingdom. It was lovingly nicknamed "The Mickyard" as a combination of Mickey Mouse and the Indianapolis Motor Speedway's nickname, The Brickyard.

The WDW Speedway closed on August 9, 2015 to make way for "transportation improvements" which meant its demolition in order to reconfigure the parking lot and entrance to the Magic Kingdom. In some years, the track was used as part of the WDW Marathon.

The track was dedicated on November 28, 1995. Indianapolis Motor Speedway Chariman of the Board, Mari Hulman George, at the earlier groundbreaking ceremony in June 1995 presented the track with one of the original paving bricks from the famous Brickyard.

Three linked ponds in the track's infield built a year after the track opened to handle drainage concerns formed the shape of Mickey Mouse's head and was dubbed Lake Mickey.

It was designed by Indianapolis Motor Speedway chief engineer Kevin Forbes originally as a venue for the Indy 200 at Walt Disney World. IndyCar, then known as the Indy Racing League, raced on the 1.0-mile tri-oval from 1996-2000. The 1996 race marked the very first event in IRL history. NASCAR also hosted Camping World Trucks Series races at the speedway in 1997 and 1998.

The venue's primary use was for the Richard Petty Driving Experience beginning in the off-season in February 1997 and was so popular that it operated roughly 365 days a year.

The high-speed attraction in Orlando was named for Richard Petty, an iconic figure in NASCAR history with multiple titles and victories. The experience allowed members of the general public to drive real NASCAR machines. In 2008, Indy Racing Experience was introduced where a guest could ride along with a professional driver.

In 2011, an Exotic Driving Experience was added that allowed car enthusiasts to drive Ferraris, Lamborghinis and Porsches on the track. Modifications were made to the speedway's infield to create an "Exotics Course".

In April 2015, guest Tavon Watson of Kissimmee participating in the Exotic Driving Experience, failed to maneuver the high-powered $240,000 Lamborghini Gallardo LP570-4 Superleggera through one of the course's curves at a speed over one hundred miles per hour, and the vehicle's right side struck a metal guardrail.

His passenger, Gary Terry, an experienced race car driver and senior operations manager at the track, was pronounced dead at the scene. Watson suffered only minor injuries. Both men were wearing seatbelts.

Florida Highway Patrol investigated the crash and determined that while the decision to run the vehicles clockwise (instead of counterclockwise like the track was designed for originally) may have factored into the incident but that it was clearly an accident and no charges were filed against the driver.

"Disney has other uses for the property, and they have the right to do with it what they want, and we respect that," Bill Scott, executive vice president of attractions operator at Petty Holdings LLC, told the *Orlando Sentinel* newspaper when the closing of the track was announced. "It's not without some sadness that we leave Walt Disney World Speedway. We had a great home here."

Downtown Disney
(1975 – 2015)

The Downtown Disney area used to be very much different than what it is today with the recent expansion into Disney Springs that features fancy new eateries and merchandise shops.

In 1974, just a few years after the opening of the Magic Kingdom, the Disney Company built a collection of vacation villas, tree house villas, and a golf course that became the Disney Village Resort.

The area would later evolve into the Disney Institute and now the Disney Vacation Club's Disney's Saratoga Springs Resort and Spa.

Black Lake—that still borders the Preview Center building, which is now the home of the Amateur Athletic Union on Hotel Plaza Boulevard—was renamed Lake Buena Vista in 1969 with incorporation of that town of the same name just up the street.

Walt Disney World actually has two small communities on property, Lake Buena Vista and Bay Lake, in order to meet the requirements necessary for WDW to be an improvement district (Reedy Creek Improvement District).

The canal system was widened into a large lake, called the Village Lagoon, next to the housing and golf course.

The name Buena Vista was chosen for its Disney connection not only to the name of the film distribution company that released the Disney films but also the name of the street in Burbank where the Disney Studios and corporate offices are located. Buena Vista is Spanish for "good view."

Right across the Village Lagoon from the Disney Village Resort was a small shopping area.

When it opened on March 22, 1975, The Lake Buena Vista Shopping Village was immediately popular with guests, locals and business people as a location where they could purchase

Disney merchandise and enjoy the Disney magic and quality service without having to pay to get into the Magic Kingdom or stay at one of the Disney resorts.

It was a quiet, soothing small-town atmosphere where visitors could leisurely dine and shop and be entertained. It was a charming retail community surrounding the lake with a barber shop, post office, art gallery, pottery shop, candle shop, and pharmacy, as well as other simple businesses.

Eventually it was renamed the Disney Village Marketplace and then it became the Downtown Disney Marketplace with the 1989 adjacent expansion into Pleasure Island, a location that mimicked the popular downtown Orlando Church Street where themed restaurants and clubs operated.

The Pleasure Island area has been recently transformed into the new Disney Springs.

The original Lake Buena Vista Shopping Village had four places to eat: Lite Bite, Heidelberger's Deli, The Village Restaurant and Cap'n Jack's (named after Disney Legend Jack Olsen who had a fondness for sailing and fishing and was instrumental in the development of Disney theme park merchandise beginning with Disneyland in 1955). All of these locations no longer exist.

Guests could also take a boat from Cruise Dock West to the Lake Buena Vista Club, where they could enjoy breakfast, lunch, and brunch, as well as French cooking at night. Entertainment from a variety of street performers as well as musical performances on the dock side stage enhanced the experience.

The Downtown Disney area was meant to be a quiet friendly oasis in the hectic and sometimes chaotic world of Disney. However, today with its transformation into Disney Springs, it is as active and often as crowded as any of the WDW theme parks.

Cap'n Jack's Restaurant

(1975 – 2013)

Cap'n Jack's Restaurant was an informal, New England-ish, nautically-themed restaurant at the Downtown Disney Marketplace on the east side. The restaurant had been a staple on the waterfront since The Lake Buena Vista Shopping Village opened in 1975.

Originally, it was called Cap'n Jack's Oyster Bar and was a location where adults could grab cocktails and appetizers in the early days of Walt Disney World. Obviously, it specialized in seafood and was one of the very few locations on or near WDW property that was open until the wee hours.

When it became an official "restaurant" around 2000 the menu expanded and featured seafood, steak, pasta dishes, and kid friendly items like chicken strips and hamburgers.

Not only was it the longest surviving original business in the Downtown Disney area, it was the last remaining Disney operated restaurant in that area as well. It was born along with now forgotten locations such as the Gourmet Pantry, the Village Spirits and so many others.

The entire area was not just a way to satisfy guests staying on Walt Disney property so that they didn't have to find transportation to downtown Orlando. It was meant to be a hub from which a housing community composed of town houses, condominiums and more would grow.

As part of the Phase Two plans for Walt Disney World property, the monorail was to be extended to stop at the shopping and dining area and some stanchion foundations were put in place and county clearances had been obtained.

Pricey shops selling elegant goods from clothes to wine were included to attract the local population as well as the tourists who could purchase items that they would be unable to find anywhere else in Orlando.

Cap'n Jack's unique hexagonal-shape offered wonderful views of the lake and Downtown Disney's marina where guests could rent watercraft to leisurely cruise the nearby waterways.

Cap'n Jack's was built out into the lagoon and was described as a "floating" restaurant. The outside porch for Cap'n Jack's was intended for live female models to walk and display the newest in swimsuits from the nearby shop, the Windjammer Dock Shop (that had a red-headed mermaid as its logo).

The restaurant was named after Disney Legend Jack Olsen who had a fondness for sailing and fishing. Olsen retired from the Disney Company in 1977 but was instrumental in shaping the Disney theme park merchandise mentality since the opening of Disneyland in 1955.

It was Olsen who jumped into dumpsters to rescue Disney animation cels, trim them into a cardboard matte and then sell them for a dollar or so to early park guests. He was the one who insisted that Disney park merchandise be distinctly different than what guests could get anywhere else.

Like many of Disney's top executives, he relocated from California to Florida to open Walt Disney World where he was the Vice President in charge of Disney Merchandise.

Cap'n Jack's last day of operation was August 17, 2013. Its closure was part of the conversion plan for the new Disney Springs and it was located approximately where the new bridge is today.

However, the name lives on at the Cap'n Jack's Margarita Bar dockside and as the name of the marina.

The famous drink at the original Cap'n Jack's Oyster Bar was the Strawberry Margarita. Actually, it was the first East Coast appearance of this type of drink but was quite popular with the California WDW cast members who had relocated to Florida and that spurred its introduction.

The World of Disney Store
(1996 -2014)

When the World of Disney store opened October 2, 1996 at Downtown Disney, its first guests were given a colorful character map to help orient themselves to the massive 51,000 square feet of retail space referred to as "The Largest Disney Character Shop in the World."

As Walt Disney World publicity described the World of Disney Store when it first opened: "It's paradise for everyone, from the newest Mickey fan to the avid Disneyana enthusiast. Disney merchandise is arranged so artfully that this remarkable store is an attraction itself. As you enter, you'll pass beneath giant airships and into lands of endless fascination.

"The journey starts in The Great Hall and 60-foot high Rotunda, where eight more fantasy airships averaging 20 feet in length are piloted by numerous Disney characters. State-of-the-art, high fidelity sound comparable only to a movie theater adds to your delight."

When the World of Disney Store originally opened, each room was given a colorful name to help more easily locate a particular item and guests were encouraged to "bring home the magic!"

Enchanted Dining Room (Candy, Gourmet Foods, Housewares, Table Top)

To the right of the Enchanted Dining Room, the Exotic Animals Room (Men's Clothing, Ties, Boxers, Hosiery). In 2006 as part of the store's 10th anniversary celebration, this room was re-themed to the Pirates of the Caribbean and Stitch and renamed the Adventure Room. Pirates in a jail cell and another outside at a steering wheel were allusions to the original ride attraction.

To the left of the Enchanted Dining Room, the Magic Room (Adult Sleepwear, Slippers, Boxers)

Straight ahead from the Enchanted Dining Room, the long hallway known as the Great Hall and Rotunda (Popular Souvenirs, Adult Apparel, Headwear, Luggage, Backpacks, Sunglasses)

Straight ahead, the Map Room (Disney Souvenirs, Stationery, Decorative Figurines, Photo Albums, Personalization)

To the right of the Map Room, the Bird Room (Women's Apparel Collections, Latest Women's Fashions)

To the left of the Map Room, the Villains Room (Disney Watches, Jewelry, Clocks, Decorative Gifts)

Straight ahead from the Map Room, the Carnival Room (Princess Costumes, Kids' Sleepwear, Dolls, Kids' Bath and Body)

To the right of the Carnival Room, the Snow White Room (Infant and Toddler Apparel, Kid's Bedding, Baby Books, Baby Plush Toys)

Straight ahead from the Carnival Room, the long final room was known as the Wonderland Room (Kids' Souvenirs, Children's Apparel, Media and Books, Plush Toys). In 2006, this room was renamed the Princess Room and was redesigned to look like a great hall in a fairy tale castle. With the opening of the Bibbidi Bobbidi Boutique there in 2006, books and media were relocated to the Map Room area.

The concept of a store "with the largest selection of Disney character merchandise in the world" was so appealing that a second, slightly smaller version of The World of Disney store opened in 2001 in the Downtown Disney shopping district at the Disneyland Resort in California.

A third site opened October 2004 within a three-story New York building that formerly housed the traditional Disney Store. It closed in late December 2009.

On July 12, 2012, another World of Disney Store opened at Disney Village in Disneyland Paris as part of a refurbishment of that area. So three World of Disney Stores are currently operating today.

With the opening of Disney Springs, the interior of The World of Disney Store was reconfigured again into an abandoned animation studio although some of the original decorative elements remain.

The Empress Lilly
(1977 – 1995)

The Lake Buena Vista Shopping Village became The Walt Disney World Village at Lake Buena Vista in 1977.

Heralding that change was the introduction of the Empress Lilly that officially opened on May 1, 1977. This paddlewheel steam ship was named after Walt Disney's widow, Lillian Bounds Disney, who was there on opening day to christen her namesake.

However, the Empress Lilly was not a boat at all despite the fact that her paddlewheel churned constantly in the early days as if she were ready to steam out of port, but a building built to resemble a boat anchored on a submerged concrete foundation. At 220 feet long by 62 feet wide, she was more than twice the size of the steamboats at the Magic Kingdom.

The Empress Lilly became home to the first Walt Disney World character breakfasts.

The upscale Empress Lounge featured a live harpist, a tradition carried on at Victoria & Albert's at the Grand Floridian Resort. The Empress Room was elegantly decorated in the style of Louis XV and men were required to wear ties and jackets to dine there just as they are today at Victoria & Albert's.

A more raucous time was had at the full bar in the Baton Rouge Lounge with comedy and Dixieland jazz by the "Riverboat Rascals" show band. The room's décor was primarily red, a visual play on the lounge's name, with the same red carpet that covered the floor of the special Lillian VIP car on the Disneyland Railroad. Lillian Disney loved the color and used it to decorate the Disney private apartment above the firehouse in Disneyland.

Above the Baton Rouge, was the Fisherman's Deck restaurant specializing in fresh fish caught daily. For those who preferred meat there was the Steerman's Quarters steakhouse restaurant with its well remembered angus beef offerings (as well as lamb and veal) while guests could look out the window at the giant churning paddlewheel.

On the third floor was the Captain's Table. Inside this private banquet hall, there was literally a 24-foot long parquet table, imported from New Orleans Square at Disneyland, which seated up to 20 guests.

During an interview in 1982, Dick Nunis revealed that the area near the Empress Lilly was to be expanded into a New Orleans section similar in style to Disneyland's New Orleans Square. The buildings would house shops on the lower level and hotel rooms on the upper levels. Apparently the storyline was now that the Empress Lilly had just pulled in to the dock to unload goods and passengers at Port Orleans.

However, this was a time of turmoil for the Disney Company so that expansion was never realized, although later a Port Orleans Resort was built not far away.

With the opening of Pleasure Island, the story behind the Empress Lilly changed once again. Now, it was the original home of the fabled Merriweather Adam Pleasure and his family and it had brought them to the island where Pleasure built his empire and permanent residence.

On April 22, 1995, the Empress Lilly closed her doors, and had the interior gutted in preparation for a new dining experience and a new owner, the Levy Restaurants who had signed a 20-year license to operate the location. The smokestacks, signage and paddlewheel were removed from the exterior, and on March 10, 1996, it reopened as Fulton's Crab House with new giant gaudy red neon signs to theme in to the rest of the Pleasure Island buildings.

DisneyQuest
(1998 – 2017)

DisneyQuest was designed to be a series of multi-story, interactive "virtual" Disney theme parks for cities around the United States.

The first five-story, one hundred thousand square foot DisneyQuest opened in the Downtown Disney West Side area on June 19, 1998 to take advantage of the participation of an already enthusiastically large audience to work out any challenges.

A second DisneyQuest opened in Chicago in 1999 but permanently closed on September 4, 2001 due to a number of factors including low attendance.

There were plans for an additional twenty other similar venues including ones in Philadelphia, the Disneyland Resort in California as well as Toronto, Canada but none of them proceeded beyond the initial planning stages.

The idea started in late 1994 with vice president of new ventures Joe DiNunzio and Mike Lang of Corporate Strategic Planning.

Ssenior producer and creative director Larry Gertz recalled:

> Since technology was arriving at a state where interactive storytelling and virtual environments were becoming possible, it seemed like a good time to push it a bit farther and develop a new kind of entertainment venue.

> The endeavor would have the environment and variety of a theme park, the interactivity of an arcade and the excitement of a thrill ride. And with the ability to create virtual environments and sets, the whole thing could be indoors and located in various cities, all over the world.

To dispel the notion that it was merely an arcade to appeal to teenaged boys, Disney hired five female show producers, three female engineers and had the lighting produced entirely by women.

Project director Pete Rahill:

> We produced fifteen different cutting edge attractions, all at once. And they all had to pass the Florida Ride Legislation review. We had to develop many technologies simultaneously that were all very different.

Disney Quest was divided into four zones of play:

- **Explore Zone**: The *Virtual Jungle Cruise, Aladdin's Magic Carpet Ride* racing through Agrabah to release the Genie and the *Pirates of the Caribbean: Battle for Buccaneer Gold.*

- **Score Zone**: A rescue mission on other planets in *Invasion! An Alien Encounter* and also *Mighty Ducks Pinball Slam*

- **Create Zone**: The *Living Easels* to paint a live masterpiece. Create and ride a virtual rollercoaster at *CyberSpace Mountain. Sid's Create-A-Toy* where guests could assemble and take home their own toy. Learn how to draw a Disney animated character at the *Animation Academy.* Create a CD by choosing from over 20 styles and 1000 vocals at the *Radio Disney SongMaker.*

- **Replay Zone**: *Buzz Lightyear's AstroBlaster* was a zany bumper car race. *Mad Wave Motion Theater* where guests rode a fantasy coaster or a high speed race car. The Dance Zone offered the latest dance video games and *KidQuest* was designed for kids ages 2 - 7.

Throughout the location, there were additional video games, pinball machines, and a Wonderland Café coffee and dessert location where guests could connect with the internet as well as a traditional Food Quest court with pizza, sandwiches, salads and other items.

The venue later included other attractions like Hercules in the Underworld, the Cybrolator, The Cave of Wonders Slide, Treasure of the Incas and Magic Mirrors. Redemption games were removed from the facility in January 2015.

In an era of smartphone apps, lifelike video games and other interactive attractions, DisneyQuest appeared too dated for many people. On June 30, 2015, Disney announced that the entire location would be closing in 2017 to make way for the NBA Experience.

Crossroads

(1988 – 2021)

If something is not physically in the theme parks or the resorts, it can be invisible to millions of Disney guests. For almost twenty years, there was a Disney owned location that some guests avoided because they didn't realize it was Disney.

The Crossroads shopping center at Lake Buena Vista where State Road 535 intersects with Hotel Plaza Boulevard was developed by the Disney Company in 1988 and then later sold off in 2005.

The 155,000-square-foot plaza's more than twenty tenants include multiple restaurants like Red Lobster, Pirate's Cove mini-golf almost hidden in the back of the complex and the region's last Gooding's supermarket.

When it opened, the McDonalds had a colorful interior decorated with authentic Disney memorabilia ranging from comic books to toys to lithographs and more. Unfortunately, they were displayed without any protection to light, heat and humidity and so when the location was updated, those items were discarded.

Jungle Jim's was a popular family restaurant filled with unusual, amusing items, including a helicopter prop from the movie *M*A*S*H* (1970), amidst the jungle décor.

Unfortunately, by 2006, the quality of service and food had dropped drastically and the restaurant had become a hangout on Monday nights for young gang members from Kissimmee. It escalated that same year with a stabbing of a young man named Cory Swift in the neck by John Feliciano over gang colors. The restaurant closed shortly thereafter and remained vacant for a long while.

While originally, there were a handful of small gift shops, today the complex is predominantly restaurant oriented and includes Buffalo Wild Wings, Quizno's, Fuddruckers, Flippers

Pizza, Dakshin Indian Cuisine, Tom and Chee, T.G.I Fridays, Sweet Tomatoes, Chevy's Mexican Restaurant, McDonald's, Uno Pizzeria & Grill, Taco Bell, Red Lobster, Noodles & Company, Moe's, Johnnies Hideaway, and Perkins.

The location provided quick and inexpensive meals for WDW cast members on their way to and from work. It also provided a nearby twenty-four hour grocery within walking distance for vacationers staying in nearby hotels.

In January 2017, it was announced that the entire area would be demolished in the next few years to make way for a reconfiguration of the area to improve the flow of traffic that often gets congested.

Traffic gets clogged on the I-4 as people try to exit onto 535. Studies show only about twenty percent of this traffic is headed toward the Disney property. Primarily, commuter traffic heading up 535 to the new residential developments north of Disney and south toward Kissimmee and Poinciana are causing much of the problem.

The interchange is not part of the I-4 expansion already under way but would be part of the next phase. However, the project has been delayed because of challenges on the I-4 expansion and the shut down of construction during the coronavirus outbreak.

The project's current design includes a feature that will take some traffic on a loop ramp that connects with Hotel Plaza Boulevard, the road leading into Disney. That ramp, an exit and drainage ponds would go on the Crossroads land.

Retail consultant David Marks, president of Marketplace Advisors, said some restaurants might be able to find another nearby place to relocate even though it would be more expensive for them, but the plaza's shutdown could also generate more business for Disney Springs.

As a result of the business shut down caused by the pandemic, many restaurants like Sweet Tomatoes closed permanently at Crossroads in 2020.

Origin of Pleasure Island

(1989 – 2008)

Church Street Station started as a downtown Orlando entertainment concept of Bob Snow in 1972. In 1985, it drew in 1.7 million visitors annually and became the fourth-largest tourist attraction in the state right behind Walt Disney World, SeaWorld, and Busch Gardens.

Among the features of Church Street Station were several unique club restaurants including Rosie O'Grady's Good Time Emporium that celebrated the happy time of the Gay Nineties and the Roaring Twenties with Rosie's Good Time Dixieland Band, bar top can-can girls and Charleston dancers. It had antique brass chandeliers, etched mirrors and leaded glass.

In addition there was the Cheyenne Saloon and Opera House that was a re-creation of an Old West saloon with the Cheyenne Stampede, country music and the Cheyenne Sweethearts.

Phineas Phogg's Dance Club was a popular dance club and the environment was decorated with memorabilia from daring balloonists both past and present. Lili Marlene's Aviator's Pub and Restaurant had authentic aviation memorabilia from both World Wars.

The Orchid Garden was a romantic setting amid wrought iron balconies and balustrades, mellow old woodwork, brick floors and stained and beveled glass. It featured live rock 'n' roll from the '50s to the '90s.

There was also Crackers Seafood Restaurant and Church Street Station Exchange, a three-story shopping emporium featuring more than fifty specialty shops and eateries in a beautiful Victorian setting.

To keep guests on Disney property instead of visiting this popular entertainment venue, at a press conference on the Empress Lilly at Downtown Disney Marketplace on July 21, 1986, Disney

CEO Michael Eisner told the press that Disney would build Pleasure Island.

It was the answer to the need for evening entertainment for guests, locals and conventions. It would be a six-acre man-made island that was scheduled to open spring 1988 and would be "a place to go when the sun goes down... in a nice Disney way" unlike the rowdy Church Street.

Attending the press conference with a model of Pleasure Island was Madame Zenobia (actress Anita Goodwin), who Eisner said would be in the Adventurers Club and "who will read your palm and tell your future". Also in attendance was old seaman Captain Spike who would be in the club Madison's Dive and tell salty stories about his love of a mermaid. Captain Spike was portrayed by Craig McNair Wilson who was artistic director of SAK theater (a well known improvisational theater group in Orlando that began in August 1977) and later helped shape the entertainment at both the Comedy Warehouse and the Adventurer's Club.

The Disney Imagineers came up with an elaborate but never fully functional or understood mythology. In 1911, wealthy adventurer Merriweather Adam Pleasure settled on the island with his family and built his own personal paradise. The disappearance of Pleasure at sea in a boating accident and a devastating hurricane in 1955 caused all of the island's buildings to fall into disrepair. In 1987, it was re-discovered by the Imagineers who re-habbed the existing structures into nightclubs.

The concept of a manufacturing district came from an idea by architect Chris Caradine who had become enamored of Granville Island in Vancouver, an industrial-fishing-manufacturing island under a huge bridge that was in the process of having the old buildings transformed into shops, theaters, restaurants, cafes, and galleries.

Pleasure Island
(1989 – 2008)

When Pleasure Island opened to help the guests understand the convoluted back story for the location devised by the Imagineers, there were twenty-six plaques placed at the entrances of the island and on the individual buildings placed there by the "Histerical" (sic) Society to explain the mythology of the island.

Walt Disney Imagineering created the back story of a Pittsburgh entrepreneur named Merriweather Adam Pleasure who arrived with his family on a Mississippi side-wheeler that steamed into Lake Buena Vista in 1911.

He envisioned a manufacturing center, research lab and development facility, as well as a social gathering spot for the famous and well-to-do. When Pleasure and his daughter disappeared on a voyage in 1941, the island fell on hard times with Hurricane Connie in 1955 inflicting near-total destruction.

The once bustling harbor community became a ghost town. But in 1987, Disney Imagineers re-discovered the island. Some buildings were renovated and some, like the Adventurers Club that had survived disaster, were reopened.

Those new businesses included Mannequins Dance Palace (with a large rotating floor and overhead mannequins attired in a variety of theatrical costumes); Neon Armadillo Saloon (a country and Western location inspired by the Cheyenne Saloon and Opera House at Church Street Station that Eisner visited and saw a huge line waiting anxiously to enter); XZFR Rockin' Rollerdrome (a dance club with a skating rink on the upper floors).

Videopolis East (a non-alcoholic club catering specifically to people younger than 21); the Fireworks Factory (a restaurant specializing in barbecue to match the "burnt" theme of a stray spark from Pleasure's cigar that had set off fireworks and blackened the interior of the building); the Portobello Yacht Club (an authentic Northern Italian cuisine restaurant to honor Pleasure's Italian wife); Merriweather's Market (a food court with four distinct sections where everything was cooked to order); the Comedy Warehouse (an improvisational comedy show with a slight "edge") and the Adventurers Club (themed as a 1930s explorer's club).

The Adventurers Club housed the many "treasures and artifacts" brought back from far off expeditions by Pleasure and his friends. Many of those artifacts were not as inanimate as they first appeared. Official club officers and members interacted with the guests the entire evening by telling stories and introducing them to the club's customs and activities.

The festivities each night included shows devoted to honorary member inductions, the Balderdash Cup competition, an episode of the radio cliffhanger *Tales of the Adventurers*, and some odd activities in the Treasure Room and Mask Room.

In addition, there were many shops unique to the location including Avigators Supply (featuring aviation and clothing merchandise with a winged alligator who was supposed to be another mascot of the Island besides the half moon-faced Funmeister); YesterEars (selling Disneyana items); Suspended Animation (selling Disney artwork) and Jessica's of Hollywood which opened in 1990 and showcased a giant two-sided neon sign of Jessica Rabbit with sequined dress and swinging leg who sat atop the light purple colored building to entice customers inside to purchase jewelry or nightgowns that featured her logo.

Disney faced many unexpected challenges running nightclubs and changes were made almost immediately. Operational issues including rowdy young gangs resulted in the location once an entrance fee was removed and the venue closed in late September 2008.

"Our decision is largely based on guest feedback," said the official Walt Disney World, "We are seeing more demand for shopping and dining experiences and less demand for clubs."

Pleasure Island New Year's Eve

(1990 – 2005)

When Pleasure Island opened, Disney felt there needed to be something to catch people's attention that this was going to be a new experience that people needed to attend every night to help generate attendance.

At one point, it was suggested that a spaceship land on Pleasure Island each night that would lead into a nightly celebration of Christmas. Merriweather Pleasure supposedly attempted to contact life in outer space and the West End Plaza had a plaque stating that Pleasure had originally intended it to be a landing platform for extraterrestrial craft.

Fortunately, wiser Disney marketing people realized that Christmas and outer space visitors didn't seem to be a good fit for the Island but that suggestion did spark the idea of celebrating New Year's Eve, a time traditionally known for partying and drinking and fireworks. So, in 1990, the Island welcomed in the New Year every night (sometimes on weekdays as early as 11 p.m.) with fireworks, confetti, professional dancers and more.

When Pleasure Island began celebrating New Year's Eve every night (a concept that was wonderfully parodied on an episode of *The Simpsons*), there was an attempt to revise the Merriweather Pleasure story. Chris Oyen, who was the show writer and director for both the Comedy Warehouse and the Adventurers Club, came up with this revision in June 1991.

On New Year's Eve in 1873, Merriweather Adam Pleasure was born. He would say later that he had been born on that day deliberately, so everyone in the world would have a reason to celebrate with him. As fate would have it, on New Year's Eve 1901, his eldest son, Stewart, was born. A plucky Merriweather claimed he had planned it that way all along. When a second son, Henry, was born on New Year's Eve, 1905, people began to believe there might be something to Merriweather's claim of orchestrating the date of his offspring's birth.

On New Year's Eve, 1911, when Pleasure steamed into Lake Buena Vista, a new chapter was opened in his life and Pleasure Island was born. When his last child, Miriam, was born on February 17, 1912, Merriweather said that it was a sign. A family tradition of landmark events occurring on New Year's Eve had been broken, and the only way to correct this chronological indiscretion was to correct time itself.

Pleasure said that since it was his island, he could say it was any day he wanted it to be. He claimed that the birth of Miriam on a date so far out of Pleasure family tradition was clearly a sign that every day should be New Year's Eve on Pleasure Island.

This, of course, meant that every night there was a New Year's Eve party on Pleasure Island. At the end of each work day, every day of the year, the laborers, artisans, inventors, and globe-trotting millionaire visitors alike, would dance in the streets as the entire Island community kicked back with wild abandon. The buildings that provided industrial functions during the daytime were reset to be dancehalls, concert or theatrical venues, or locations for dining or refreshments. Every night there was a fireworks display, choreographed by Pleasure himself.

It is in honor of this spirit of unabated whimsy and dedication to unrelenting fun that the tradition of a nightly New Year's Eve Party had been restored to Pleasure Island. With the removal of the West End and Hub stages and other changes in early 2006, it brought an end to the celebrations.

Ear Force One

(1986 – 2006)

Ear Force One was created for Walt Disney World's 15th anniversary in 1986. It was a gigantic ten story high hot-air balloon in the shape of Mickey Mouse's head that was inspired by the much smaller helium Mickey Mouse balloons sold in the Disney parks.

Ear Force One measured 96 feet from the bottom of its basket to the top of Mickey's head. Each ear was 35 feet in diameter, his nose snout was 33 feet long, each eye 16.5 feet high and the 54.6 foot diameter head measured 168.3 feet in circumference. Un-inflated and minus the basket, the balloon weighed roughly 330 pounds.

The huge mouse-eared balloon was manufactured by Cameron Balloons Ltd. of Bristol, England, noted for producing many odd-shaped balloons since 1971.

A typical hot air balloon is made up of about 200 pieces of special purpose nylon fabric drawn from six to 20 patterns. Ear Force One was much more complicated, with 500 pieces drawn from 50 patterns. The pilots for that first tour were Robert Carlton and David Justice. Ear Force One also toured the nation (including visiting Disneyland) in 1988 to celebrate Mickey's 60th birthday that year.

To celebrate the 50th anniversary of Disneyland, a newer version of the original Ear Force One (that had been decommissioned many years earlier) was created by Cameron Balloons and was dubbed "The Happiest Balloon on Earth" in 2006. It was unique because Mickey sported a Golden Ears souvenir cap like the one guests could purchase at Disneyland.

The balloon was approximately 113,000 cubic feet in volume. It stood 98-feet tall and spanned 53 feet from ear-to-ear.

Since Mickey's nose is 5.5 feet in diameter, an average child could easily stand up inside it. 2,000 averaged-sized children could easily fit inside the inflated balloon. If Mickey's proportionate body were added to the balloon he would stand more than 200 feet tall.

During the tour, the system was moved in a Ford F-250 and trailer from location to location. It was the first hot air balloon to ever rise over the Grand Canyon. Even more impressively, it flew below the rim of the Grand Canyon on April 11, 2006, a much trickier maneuver due to air currents.

It was built for a 14-stop tour, including cities like San Francisco to showcase the balloon against the backdrop of the Golden Gate Bridge.

After the last stop on the tour, July 17, 2006 at Disneyland the balloon was returned to Cameron Balloons for removal of the souvenir Gold Cap, a project that was called "Back to Black."

It now resides in a warehouse in Boise, Idaho and is kept "ready for flight" condition because as one of the most popular designs of such balloons, many invitation requests come in from local festivals and balloon rallies. It participated daily in Leon, Guanajuato (Mexico) from November 16-19, 2012 for the 11th annual International Balloon Festival, in Metropolitan Ecological Park.

In 1987, Donald Duck had a hot-air balloon created of his likeness dubbed the Zip-A-Dee-Doo Duck. To kick off the New Year in 1988, the Zip-A-Dee-Doo Duck joined Ear Force One on New Year's Day bringing two big Disney stars to the Magic Kingdom Park sky.

In 1991 to celebrate the 20th anniversary of Walt Disney World, Cameron Balloons created the "Castle in the Sky" balloon that featured the WDW castle floating on a huge puffy cloud that had the logo "Walt Disney World 20 Years."

LiMOUSEine
(1989 – 1996)

In the spring of 1989, to promote the May first opening of the Disney-MGM Studios, the "LimMOUSEine" with a costumed Mickey Mouse and Walt Disney World Ambassador Kathleen Sullivan, departed Orlando on March 5, 1989, for an almost-40 city East Coast tour, beginning in Indianapolis that would last for roughly four months.

The driver of the unique burgundy stretch limo was Bill Marable, a former Disney bus driver, who often had to maneuver through narrow and awkward turns during the trip. The 9,000 pound, six-wheeled forty foot long vehicle was loaded with high technology, since it was supposed to represent Mickey's "home away from home".

The weight was about 7,980 pounds, but the electronics added approximately 1,000 pounds. Overall length was 40 feet with overall width being 79.5 inches. The height was 65 inches with a wheelbase of 331 inches.

This five-door vehicle sat a dozen passengers comfortably, but was placed low to the ground to accommodate the size of the costumed Disney characters that sometimes included Minnie Mouse and Roger Rabbit as well as Mickey. There were yards of windows and four oversized glass sunroofs with sliding shades, large enough for the characters to stand up and wave to guests.

This super limo, billed as "the longest fixed-frame vehicle that can be driven legally on U.S. roads," included electronic gear (much of it donated by Sony and considered top-of-the-line at the time). The base vehicle for the LiMOUSEine was a Lincoln Town Car cut in half, and stretched more than 20 feet on a beefed-up frame.

The interior included an entertainment center with AM-FM stereo cassette player, CD player, 20 speakers, 8mm videocassette player, a half-inch Beta videocassette player and two eight-inch Trinitron color monitors with wireless remote. Passengers could watch television programs received by antenna or watch videos. Two cellular telephones with separate lines could be used from four different locations in the car.

Perched atop the grille, and looking remarkably (but not intentionally, a Disney spokesman insisted, because that would violate intellectual property rights) like a version of the Rolls-Royce "Spirit of Ecstasy" hood ornament was a 24-karat gold-plated Tinker Bell figure with her wings stretched behind her.

The Rolls-Royce front end with gold-plated radiator shell and trim had a 24-karat Mickey three-circled head shape. There were custom-built Mickey ears over front wheel wells, sparkling shooting-star effects on both front doors, 12 external parade speakers for parades and drive-up fanfares (with 1,200 watts of amplifier), red carpet and hook-ups for external power when parked with engine off.

Designed by Disney artist Tom Tripodi, at a cost of more than $100,000, the LiMOUSEine was built by Ultra Corp. of Brea, California, from a potpourri of car parts. Ultra was renown for building limos for celebrities.

It appeared in the Citrus Bowl Parade in Florida on January 1, 1990, with Mickey Mouse, Minnie Mouse and Roger Rabbit standing up and waving through individual sun roofs.

Barbie arrived at her "Magical World of Barbie" show at Epcot's World Showcase in 1994 in the LiMOUSEine that had been repainted pink with metallic sparkles and included Barbie memorabilia inside. Devoted fans could meet both Ken and Barbie and have their pictures taken with them outside the car. The show ended in 1995.

With another paint job, the limo reappeared driving down Main Street U.S.A. at the Magic Kingdom for Walt Disney World's 25th anniversary in 1996. It then ended up in the "boneyard" of Disney-MGM Studios Backlot Tour for awhile and was eventually placed in storage.

STOLport
(1971 – CIRCA 2000)

While driving toward the Magic Kingdom, guests often wonder about a paved area off the right side of the road that has sometimes been used for overflow parking, training bus drivers, temporary storage of a variety of items, and the staging of the tracks of the Magic Kingdom's Seven Dwarfs Mine Train attraction.

That area was actually an operating airfield known as STOLport (Short Take Off and Landing) for smaller propeller planes. The very first official United States STOLport was the one at Walt Disney World that opened on October 17, 1971 on that unique area to the side of the road. The official dedication ceremony was at a luncheon on October 22, 1971.

Shawnee Airlines operated scheduled passenger service between the Lake Buena Vista STOLport (sometimes referred to as the Walt Disney World Airport or by the desigination "DWS", Disney World STOLport, in its earliest days) and Orlando McCoy Jetport (it did not become Orlando International Airport until 1976) as well as the Tampa International Airport. For these short hops, Shawnee used nineteen deHavilland Canada DHC-6 Twin Otter turboprop planes.

Shawnee's intrastate flights to fourteen Florida cities were so popular that major airlines eventually moved into key Shawnee markets, prompting a shutdown of Shawnee on December 28, 1972. As a result, commercial service to STOLport was discontinued as well and never resumed because it was considered a failed experiment.

Executive Airlines and Volusia Aviation Service also utilized in a limited fashion STOLport for the first few months through January 1972 and then stopped operation. WDW's STOLport was utilized not only by a handful of tourists but also celebrities, politicians, and Disney executives.

From a 1972 advertisement:

> Shawnee Airlines....your magic carpet into Walt Disney World.
>
> Now Shawnee has nine daily shuttle flights from McCoy Jetport, Orlando to the Vacation Kingdom of the World. When you deplane from your STOL flight, you are within three minutes of the Walt Disney World hotels, Magic Kingdom theme park, and the Golf Resort. Only $7.00 per person –for more information, ask your travel agent or Eastern Airlines representative.

The reason it told people to contact Eastern Airlines was because that carrier was the official airline of Walt Disney World so tourists landing at the McCoy Jetport on an Eastern Airlines flight could make an almost instant connection for the hop to STOLport and vice versa.

WDW's STOLport was meant to be the beginning of an interstate STOL transportation system and while a handful of other STOLports were opened in the U.S. in the early 1970s, they were usually for private use or testing only. The craze for STOLports was short-lived and for the most part ceased to exist by the turn of the current century.

The airfield had very few facilities, one of the reasons for its demise, like hangars to protect planes from the Florida weather. At most, the airport could only handle perhaps a maximum of four aircraft at a time although it never had that many planes operating there.

Construction of the monorail extension in 1980 to Epcot made using STOLport even more difficult for pilots. The airport was still listed as a private airfield by the FAA through the end of the 1990s but ceased being listed as such by 2004.

Over the years, a handful of buildings were added in the area including fairly recently two with the image of Sorcerer Mickey on them meaning that they are temporary field offices for Imagineers who are supervising some new construction or development somewhere nearby.

The Golf Resort/Disney Inn

(1986 – 1996)

The Golf Resort was originally a building located in the middle of the Palm and Magnolia golf courses. It was designed to look like a two story country clubhouse and did not have any guest rooms.

Guest wings were added in 1973 as part of Walt Disney World's Phase 2 expansion. It retained the name The Golf Resort but was not generally considered a WDW resort because of its small size and not being on the monorail loop among other things.

In February 1986, Disney expanded the resort and renamed it The Disney Inn in hopes of attracting more than just golfers, promoting it as having the intimate and rustic charm of a quiet country inn. It was mildly re-themed to Snow White and the Seven Dwarfs in hopes of reinforcing the Disney connection.

In 1996, the resort was purchased by the U.S. Department of Defense for $43 million for use in the MWR (Morale, Welfare and Recreation) program and limited the resort to eligible active and retired military personnel although Disney still owns the land on which the resort sits. The resort was renamed Shades of Green because at the time all military fighting uniforms had some shade of green.

My friend Rich Cullen who still works at WDW worked the front desk of the Disney Inn during its last three years of existence and generously shared some of his memories of the resort.

Rich Cullen: "It is my understanding that when people heard the name 'Golf Resort' they thought they had to be golfers to stay there. The story goes that when the name was changed to The Disney Inn and a Snow White theme was created, occupancy went up significantly, not just people who couldn't get into the Contemporary or the Polynesian.

"The rooms were large compared to other Disney resorts, a little less than 500 square feet as I recall. The newer rooms were brighter and the decor had a cottage charm with details like an oak headboard but nothing crazy in terms of a Snow White/ Dwarfs theme. There were just subtle touches that didn't hit you over the head. The wonderful sign at our entrance was a yawning Sleepy holding a candle as if he was going off to bed and that logo was on everything.

"Most of the remodeled rooms had a framed original muted color print that included some images of objects relating to the story of Snow White. The rooms had two queen beds and a pull out love seat as well as a small round table with two chairs. Some of the rooms had King beds which we commonly reserved for honeymooners.

"Three types of room view categories: Garden View, Golf Course View (both of which were roughly $185 during the regular season) and Pool View (that was $195 during the regular season).

"The Garden Gallery was the main restaurant right off of our lobby and it served breakfast, lunch and dinner. Their specialty was "fried ice cream" which was similar to the fried ice cream that was popular at the Mexican chain restaurant called Chi-Chi's.

"We still served a lot of golfers. There were actually three golf courses. The Palm, The Magnolia and a great nine hole walking course called Oak Trails. There were two swimming pools at the Inn with the large family pool being in the shape of Mickey Mouse's head. I have so many fond memories of working there but the cast members I work with today don't know it even existed!"

Disney Institute

(1996 – 2002)

CEO Michael Eisner and his family visited the Chautauqua Institution in 1985 in upstate New York that offered lectures, performances, recreation, and, most specifically, classes designed for adults to enhance their education during the summer months. Eisner felt this would be a great idea to build at Walt Disney World and would attract older, more affluent guests who were not interested in the theme parks.

In order to save on costs on the venture, it was decided to convert the already existing Lake Buena Vista villas and townhouses and just build the additional classroom facilities there.

The new structures were designed by Tom Beedy and given the look of a small, friendly New England town. Facilities at the 457-room lakeside resort were designed to accommodate about 900 people at its peak, a fairly modest number considering the other resorts and attendance at the theme parks.

New structures included a 38,000-square-foot two-story sports and fitness center with a full basketball court, indoor pool, and a full-service spa with seaweed facial or an "aroma therapy" massage; a 225-seat Performance Center that was acoustically perfect and featured side boxes in the audience; a 400-seat movie theater without a balcony; and a 1,150-seat uncovered amphitheater (which proved to be a huge mistake when it rained or the Orlando sun and heat were too intense so could not be used).

Some upgrades to the Lake Buena Vista living accommodations were made, but most of these were merely cosmetic, so there was no outlet to plug in and recharge any devices like a computer. The prices were the same as the premium resorts on property but without the same amenities which caused guest complaints.

The Disney Institute opened on February 9, 1996 with the motto "You won't believe what you can do!"

Too often guests stayed at other resorts and simply drove in to attend classes or performances. The classrooms were designed to be small for an intimate experience but even with a full classroom it was not enough to cover the cost of the overhead for instructors, materials, maintenance and more.

When D.I. opened in 1996, guests could choose from more than 80 programs in nine different program track areas, including Entertainment Arts (which also encompassed all the animation classes), Sports and Fitness, Life Styles, Story Arts (with classes like *As Walt Would Tell It*), Culinary Arts, Design Arts, Environment (including a class where guests could make their own mini-Mickey Mouse topiary), Performing Arts (with a radio and television studio) and Youth Programs. Within six months many of these classes were cut with only the more popular ones surviving and another round of massive cuts came in 1997. The Disney Institute in its first year of existence had the highest guest satisfaction ratings on all of WDW property for its class experiences.

Individual classes were each offered generally twice or three times a week (usually every other day) and were roughly two to three hours long. There was a morning session and an afternoon session. There was a two hour break for lunch and in the evening there were events either in the Performance Center or the Cinema.

Eventually, the guest enrichment programs slowly disappeared entirely and Disney Institute closed as a physical location in 2002. The Disney Institute still exists today in name offering expensive business classes to corporate clients throughout the world.

Many things on the site were gutted and razed when the area was transformed into the Saratoga Springs resort that opened on May 17, 2004.

Fort Wilderness: River Country

(1976 – 2001)

River Country! Big River Country.
It's a hoot. It's a holler! It's a water jamboree!
River Country. Big River Country.
If you're hot around the collar it's the cool place to be!

That was the opening verse of a 1977 song written about Walt Disney World's a themed water park called Disney's River Country on that opened June 20, 1976 as part of the Fort Wilderness Resort on the shore of Bay Lake.

Originally, this water park was going to be called "Pop's Willow Grove" and was meant to be reminiscent of "an old fishing hole" from the time period of Tom Sawyer and Huck Finn with items like rope swings enhancing that story.

River Country was about one-fourth the size of Typhoon Lagoon since the Disney Company had no idea whether such a then radical idea would be successful.

Attractions included a 330,000 gallon clear water pool called Upstream Plunge, Slippery Slide Falls, two sixteen foot rock slides with faux rock work (scattered with pebbles from streambeds in Georgia and the Carolinas) done by Imagineer Fred Joerger who did rock work on everything from the Jungle Cruise's Schweitzer Falls to Big Thunder Mountain, and the Ol' Swimmin' Hole dedicated by President Gerald Ford's daughter, Susan.

The Ol' Swimmin' Hole had Whoop-n-Holler Hollow, two long winding chutes that ended with a splashing entry into the water.

Water from nearby Bay Lake was pumped through the inside of River Country's artificial mountain to the top of the flumes and raft ride at the rate of 8,500 gallons a minute and then eventually through the miracle of gravity spilled back into the lake.

There was a natural soft sand beach underfoot the massive pool rather than a concrete bottom which was a unique innovation at the time.

Even with the filtration system, the water from the lake was not completely purified and that caused some red flags for Disney Legal.

Its huge popularity resulted in many sold out days since the Walt Disney World water park had limited capacity. It became apparent that a larger water park facility was needed but it took just over a decade for it to become a reality.

Typhoon Lagoon opened on June 1, 1989 just across the street from the newly built Pleasure Island and was home to the world's largest outdoor surf pool (not just a wave pool). That new water park also proved popular so in 1995, Blizzard Beach was opened to accommodate the demand.

These new options led to a drop in attendance at the more difficult to access River Country. In 1998, the water park tried to compete with the "All-American Water Party" promotion where every day was celebrated as the Fourth of July with games, Disney characters in country costumes, live country music and good old fashioned barbeque.

In September 2001, River Country quietly closed at the end of the summer season and never re-opened. In 2002, Walt Disney World spokesman Bill Warren told the Orlando Sentinel newspaper that River Country could be reopened "if there's enough guest demand".

Supposedly, River Country could not claim the honor of being America's first water park, a designation given to Wet and Wild that opened in 1977, because it was considered not a separate park but an extension of the resort.

The decaying ruins of the innovative water park remained for nearly two decades. In 2018, it was announced that the site would become a new DVC propery with 900 rooms that would open in 2022.

Fort Wilderness Railroad

(1974 – 1980)

The Fort Wilderness Resort and Campground opened on November 19, 1971 and was much larger than most campgrounds at the time, so trams, bicycles and busses provided guests with transportation options but were not enough. The official opening of the Fort Wilderness Railroad was January 1, 1974.

The railroad was considered a Disney attraction, and was promoted accordingly on marketing material, even charging guests a minimal fee of fifty cents per day (later a dollar) to use it. This made Fort Wilderness the only Disney resort, so far, that had an attraction. It lasted roughly six years until February 1980.

The railroad consisted of four steam trains, each pulling five cars, around a circular route through the campground at a maximum speed of ten miles an hour. Each engine ran on steam and used diesel fuel to stoke the fire. The track was approximately twice the length of the track at the Magic Kingdom Park.

A single train was roughly about 150 feet long and could seat up to 90 guests.

The trains were smaller than the ones at the Magic Kingdom and were based on the traditional Baldwin "plantation locomotives" popular in the Hawaiian islands.

The railroad used a smaller gauge track (30 inches between the rails on the track) than at the Magic Kingdom (36 inches) which may have influenced people into thinking that the train itself was scaled smaller but it was full-sized.

Unlike every other Disney train (even the ones operating on Big Thunder Mountain Railroad), none of the engines were ever named. They were only numbered, and each of the four engines had a distinctive icon on the headlamps: elk, bison, deer and ram.

In the beginning, the train ran from 8 a.m. to 9 p.m. everyday causing some complaints from guests who disliked the fact that at all grade crossings the extremely loud whistle would sound. Eventually, the trains would cease operation around 5 p.m. eliminating that problem.

With the opening of River Country in May 1976, the train became the favored mode of transportation. New additions had to be made to the train cars like rubber floors, because of the dripping wet guests who had enjoyed Disney's first water park.

The Disney Company never gave an official explanation or even an official closing date. The railroad was simply put on "hiatus" early in 1980.

Some claimed that safety was an issue and that the nearness of the tracks to the guests made Disney Legal fearful. Some claimed that it was just too expensive to operate and could never recover its costs.

The bottom line is that since the track was not laid correctly in the first place that even with attempts to make adjustments, the basic problem still existed that could not be overcome without a hefty investment.

After years of being outside and subjected to Florida heat and humidity, the engines and the coach cars were sold off to private collectors who restored them. All of the engines are now in California. Former Disney Executive John Lasseter has an engine and a couple of coach cars in his backyard railroad in Northern California.

Two of the coach cars were modified and placed temporarily at the entrance of Pleasure Island as ticket booths. One of those coaches is now at the front of Typhoon Lagoon, and the other was auctioned off. Four of the cars and 3,000 feet of track were donated to the Brevard Zoo in Melbourne, Florida, but over the years those coaches found other homes.

Fort Wilderness: Lawnmower Tree

(1971 – 2013)

For decades, a natural wonder delighted guests at Fort Wilderness Resort and Campground. Every time guests would visit they would seek out this living curiosity to see how it had changed over the intervening time since their last visit and were always surprised.

Years before Walt Disney World ever opened someone who lived in the area had leaned an old, push-style blade lawnmower up against a tree and left it there. No one seems to know who that person was or why they left the lawnmower there.

The tree grew through the tool so it was absorbed and became part of the tree's gnarled roots above the ground with significant rusting parts sticking out prominently.

When a tree is growing, and it encounters something that gets in the way of its growth, it can do three things: stop growing, grow away from it, or grow around it.

As the area was being developed for the campground, it was discovered by WDW Imagineers who thought it looked interesting and decided to leave it as a hidden treasure curiosity rather than remove it.

It was located just off the sidewalk about five feet from the path about halfway between Pioneer Hall and the marina about a hundred feet off the lake.

The Imagineers even decided to create a back story to explain its existence and integrate it into the lore of the campground. They installed a sign next to it that read:

> Too long did Billy Bowlegs
> Park his reel slow mower
> Alas, one warm and sunny day
> Aside a real fast grower.

So the lawnmower tree was a popular landmark at the resort since its opening in November 1971.

As the decades passed, more and more of the lawnmower disappeared into the tree as it expanded until roughly 2007 when just a few rusting blades were still visible at the foot of the tree.

By then, the tree was dead, either through natural causes or having most of the upper half of the tree cut off. Anyway, only about twelve feet of the trunk remained and the tree had stopped absorbing the remains of the lawnmower.

Disney Legal determined that the rusty remains provided a possible safety hazard since guests sometimes would go up and touch the parts.

The Walt Disney Company hired an outside contractor to quietly remove the tree in late October 2013 without alerting the guests.

The tree was so well known that it was listed in the earliest Birnbaum Official Guides to Walt Disney World as "a point of interest worth hunting down" and continued to be listed into the 21st Century editions.

The Walt Disney Company itself promoted the lawnmower tree as a "fun fact" on official handouts to the media and it appeared on the earliest campground maps.

Over the years, of all the WDW resorts, Ft. Wilderness has experienced the most removals of significant landmarks that were enjoyed by countless guests over the decades including the famous railroad, the first water park River Country, the petting zoo that had Minnie Moo the cow with the black three-circled Mickey Mouse imprint on her side, food trucks and other things.

Fort Wilderness: Minnie Moo

(1990 – 2001)

Mickey Moo, a white Holstein cow with a black Mickey Mouse head silhouette shape naturally occurring on her side, was housed in Big Thunder Ranch at Disneyland's Frontierland in 1988. Mickey Moo was a part of Mickey's 60th birthday celebration that year but became instantly a popular attraction for guests.

The unusual marking on the side of the cow was not quite as unusual as it was originally assumed. A Midwest farmer contacted the Walt Disney Company with photos of his own cow that had the same type of Mickey Mouse silhouette head.

Minnie Moo, named after Mickey's girlfriend, came to the Walt Disney World Resort from Edgerton, Minnesota, in 1990, living first in the Magic Kingdom. Grandma Duck's Petting Farm operated at Mickey's Birthdayland/Mickey's Starland from 1988-1996. In 1996, the area was transformed into The Barnstormer at Goofy's Wise Acres Farm.

With this change in the area, Minnie Moo and the other animals were moved to a Petting Farm at the Tri-Circle D Ranch (near the Pony Rides) in Disney's Fort Wilderness Resort and Campground. Minnie Moo died in August 2001, at the age of fifteen, a little more than the average lifespan for a cow.

The Disney Company did not release a notice of her death, because John McClintock, the Disney spokesman at the time, said "it was too sensitive" a subject. Just as Disney never officially revealed to guests that the 400-pound spotted grouper named Orson at Epcot's Living Seas pavilion went to the big seafood buffet in the sky.

The animals were sequestered in their pens for the health and safety of both the guests and the animals but were clearly visible. The petting farm was officially closed early in 2005 with the animals relocated to Disney's Animal Kingdom's Affection Section.

To debunk a Disney Urban Myth, there was only one Minnie Moo (and only one Mickey Moo). Many people claim that there were multiple Minnies over the years, but that is not true. When they died, the Disney Company did not contemplate replacing them.

It was estimated that millions of adults and children visited Minnie Moo, petted her, talked to her and took her photo. She was prominently used in publicity material, although she was occasionally confused with Mickey Moo who remained on the west coast.

A memorial plaque for Minnie Moo was placed on the wall on the right-hand side in the trophy room (now the Walt Disney Horse Museum room) at the barn at Disney's Fort Wilderness Resort & Campground but was removed quite some years ago. Below it were photos of some of the animals at the petting zoo, including goats and "Chester" the pig that have also been removed.

"Minnie Moo brought much joy to both our guests and our Cast Members," said Tom Hopkins, animal operations director for Animal Programs, at the time of her death of natural causes. "We will miss her greatly."

The popularity of Mickey Moo and Minnie Moo sparked a short-lived frenzy where the Disney Company was inundated with offers of various animals that had a Mickey Mouse type marking on them, from pigs and dogs to even inanimate objects like potatoes.

In January 1991, Walt Disney World purchased an Iowa pig named Mickey from Tom and Teresa Reuter of Monticello that had three linked black spots that resembled the silhouette of Mickey Mouse's head. They also took a brother piglet with similar markings. Mickey Pig and Mickey Piglet joined Minnie Moo for many years at the Petting Farm.

Discovery Island
(1974 – 1999)

The Walt Disney Company bought Riles Island in Bay Lake in 1965 and Walt intended for it to be called Blackbeard's Island to theme in with the movie *Blackbeard's Ghost* (1968).

In early 1973, the Disney Company announced that the island would be named "Treasure Island" after the 1950 Disney live action feature film and would have walkways, small lakes and waterfalls available to "explorers and picnickers." Plans were made to build some physical locations from the film and novel and house nearly 600 rare tropical birds on the island.

On April 8, 1974, after the Walt Disney Company used 15,000 cubic yards of soil and 500 tons of boulders and 500 tons of trees to transform the landscape, "Treasure Island" opened to the public. It was a sanctuary for dozens of birds, reptiles, mammals and other non-avian species.

There was also a beached ship, but not the *Hispaniola*. It was the remains of Captain Flint's ship, the *Walrus*, according to the original map.

That early Walt Disney World map of the island for guests proclaimed: "Sail the Seven Seas of Walt Disney World to an island filled with tropic beauty, colorful birds, and the mystery of Ben Gunn's buried treasure!" Cast members wore appropriately themed pirate wardrobe and the name of locations around the island included Jolly Roger Wharf, Buccaneer's Cove, Doubloon Lagoon, Mutineer Falls, Skeleton Island, Black Dog Swamp, Scavenger Beach, Rum Point and the Mizzen Mast.

The reverse side of the tri-fold map claimed that some of the future attractions would include:

- **Billy Bones's Dilemma**: Captain Flint's first mate falls prey to the perils of the open sea.

- **The Blockhouse**: Site of the battle for the treasure map. "Though fully armed... we were still out-numbered by Long John Silver's buccaneers!"
- **Spy Glass Hill**: A fantastic group of rocks in the heart of the island. In this primeval playground, you'll discover the secrets of this treasure isle!
- **Ben Gunn's Cave**: As mysterious as the strange hermit himself. Its exact location is unknown even today... but we know it's someplace on the island!
- **Wreck of the *Hispaniola***: This seagoing vessel led by Captain Smollet, once anchored here in search of buried treasure... only to be overtaken by her mutinous crew, headed by the self-appointed captain, Long John Silver! She was later run ashore by the brave young Jim Hawkins... never to sail again!"

The island would resemble a more adult version of the iconic Tom Sawyer Island in the Magic Kingdom with plenty of "natural" wonders to explore, as well as a mystery to be solved.

The island could be accessed for a half-day experience by either taking a direct motor launch from a resort dock or as part of the "Walt Disney World Cruise," a tour of the Seven Seas Lagoon and Bay Lake that stopped at the island.

For unknown reasons, a pirate theme for the island was eventually abandoned and the island was renamed yet again. It was called Discovery Island roughly three years later, around 1977, and became an official zoological park accredited by the American Association of Zoological Parks and Aquariums.

It closed to the public on April 8, 1999, and during the next three months the wildlife was relocated to Disney's Animal Kingdom in a hub area that was rechristened Discovery Island. Disney claimed that lagging attendance, some maintenance issues and the fact that DAK was better equipped to handle the welfare of the animals contributed to the island's closing.

Polynesian Village: The Eastern Winds
(1971 – 1978)

When Walt Disney World opened, only four monorails meant to be the primary transportation to the Magic Kingdom and the resorts were operating and could not handle the capacity crowds.

Emergency trams that frequently broke down were immediately put into service to transport guests from the parking lot to the entrance as well as any water craft including the keel boats from Frontierland that could ferry guests across the Seven Seas Lagoon to the main entrance.

That included calling into service two specially built temperamental side-wheeler steamboats, *The Southern Seas* and the *Ports-O-Call* that had been built for leisurely "Moonlight Cruises" through the waterways or special evening charter parties with alcohol served by two or three hostesses from the Contemporary Resort.

When the Magic Kingdom closed for the night, there wasn't much for adults to do other than the Top of the World musical show on the top floor of the Contemporary. The plan was to have some watercraft for adult evening cruises to offer guests who still wanted to do something on property.

The Eastern Winds, a cocktail lounge aboard an authentic 65-foot Chinese Junk, was docked at the Polynesian Resort from 1971 to 1978. It was available for charters, and took a crew of two to operate: a pilot and a deckhand.

The ship included a galley on board for dining as well as a full wet bar. Often during charters, the crew would also include a chef, a server, a bartender as well as a cocktail waitress. The large wheel was located in the stern of the 50,000-pound boat and took 22 turns from lock to lock.

It was built in Hong Kong in 1964, and was later purchased by a Texas oil baron. Football legend Joe Namath did own it at one time as well.

As Bill "Sully" Sullivan who helped open WDW in 1971 told me:

> There was a real Chinese junk out there in the lagoon and people could rent that boat and take it out for parties. I remember one of the problems was the Disney art directors wanted to paint it but the wood was teak. You can't paint teak because then it can't breathe and the whole thing just rotted. It just stunk to high heavens.

> Pete Crimmings bought that boat down in Miami somewhere, I think. It was somebody's personal playhouse and there was just a big mattress on the top deck. We had to change all that but it looked great.

Ron Cooper and his partner Court Glanadorp were flying in a private plane over Florida and spotted the junk sitting anchored in the Seven Seas Lagoon. Disney has discontinued the cruises and left it in the lagoon as a decoration because it was too much trouble to remove. Cooper made an offer to buy it and within a month, Disney accepted.

However, time and weather had taken its toll on the craft and it was in terrible shape. All the incidentals had been stripped and the varnish was off.

The ship could not be floated anywhere so a trailer had to be positioned under the craft and it was transported along the interstate with much fanfare. When it arrived at its new home, it was launched off the back of the trailer because a crane operator refused to lift it for fear of further damage.

After two years spent refurbishing the boat, it was used for pleasure cruises in St. Thomas in the U.S. Virgin Islands.

Boardwalk: Seashore Sweets/ Flying Fish Café
(1996 - 2016)

To accommodate the new AbracadaBar at the Boardwalk Inn and Villas, an old fashioned ice cream and candy shop called Seashore Sweets was closed February 1, 2016. The shop was especially known for offering hand-scooped ice cream.

Seashore Sweets had a main story related to the Miss America Pageant that was celebrated throughout this location as well as a smaller tangent story about a well-known candy associated with Atlantic City.

Atlantic City is where saltwater taffy was created in 1883 when a clever businessman named David Bradley sold some taffy that had a hint of salt water when his shop was flooded by ocean water. Salt water is not an ingredient in salt water taffy today. Of course, salt water taffy could be purchased in Seashore Sweets usually with Goofy's face on the bag.

The main storyline was that two sisters, known as the "Sweet Sisters", who competed in the early Miss America pageant decided to stay in the area and opened the shop. Their picture was on the outside sign and the motto of the store was "Confections served with Affection" (heart shapes in the letter "O" in that sign).

Atlantic City was famous for the Miss America pageant that began in the 1920s and lasted for 85 years on the Boardwalk before relocating to Las Vegas in 2007. It later returned to Atlantic City in 2013.

There were many authentic artifacts from those pageants like souvenir programs and tickets inside the store including in a transparent case on the right hand side of the entrance with a trophy, crown, regal cape and scepter used in an actual Miss America pageant.

Up above near the ceiling were framed photos of all the Miss America winners from 1921 through 2007 (when it stopped being held in Atlantic City).

In the earliest days, the women were not just judged in a swimsuit competition (called the Bathers' Revue) but also as part of the Rolling Chair Parade, referenced in a newspaper article on the wall.

Framed posters and memorabilia could be found in every area of the small shop. A souvenir program from the 1942 pageant would have cost twenty-five cents that year but is worth many times that price today.

The inspiration for the name Flying Fish Café next door that opened in 1996 most likely came from a classic Coney Island roller coaster called the Flying Turns. One of the ride vehicles was called the Flying Fish.

The interior of the restaurant was originally a colorful homage to Coney Island. The back of the booths resembled the curving lifts and drops of a roller coaster. On the back wall was a huge depiction of a back-lit Ferris wheel.

Fish did, in fact, fly overhead in pairs in the restaurant on a version of the famous parachute ride that was a decades-long favorite at Steeplechase Park at Coney Island. In fact one of the first images on the wall mural is of people riding the eight wooden horses on a steel track at Steeplechase. On the cloud painted ceiling, the stars changed colors every few minutes.

The entire interior, including the addition of a different on-stage kitchen and expanded dining space for private events, was redesigned in a 2016 renovation. The name was changed from Café to restaurant.

The new upscale design includes images of flying fish in a chandelier of glass, the kitchen tiles and the upholstery. The restaurant also had references to the classic boardwalk with carnival art, vintage carnival games and more.

WDW Christmas Traditions

Walt Disney World once had several holiday traditions that were unique to the Disney theme park including the Jolly Holidays Dinner Show and The Glory and the Pageantry of Christmas show.

The Jolly Holidays Dinner Show at Disney's Contemporary Resort was performed from 1992 through the 1998 Christmas season when it was discontinued. The Fantasia Ballroom was converted into an immersive theater-in-the-round setting with more than a hundred talented performers in a musical extravaganza. Besides the raised main stage, there were several smaller stages on the outer perimeter of the tables.

"Those Jolly, Jolly, Jolly Holidays! Those Holly, Holly, Holly Jolly Days! All the decorations! Many celebrations! Many happy faces! Cozy fireplaces! Let the bells ring out now! Everyone sing out now!"

Performers spilled out into the audience, as well. The show took place at "Holiday Village" where the patriarch of the town known simply as "Papa" (and looking a bit like a grey-bearded Sebastian Cabot with a deep gravely voice) recalled his memories of the holidays.

Mickey, Minnie, Pluto, Goofy and Chip'n'Dale cavorted with perky singers and dancers. The Country Bears dropped by to play a tune before they went back out into the snow to play. There was even a short version of the *Nutcracker Suite* featuring the hippos and ostriches from *Fantasia*. Of course, some scenes seemed to be borrowed from other shows including the tap dancing horses for the sleigh ride, the marching toy soldiers and Santa Goofy making an appearance.

In addition, guests enjoyed an all-you-can-eat feast of fresh-cooked turkey, honey baked ham and other holiday treats. It was a hugely popular show, often completely sold out even at a premium price, although significant changes were made in its final year that did not please everyone.

For more than fifteen years in the 1980s and 1990s, the Disney Village Marketplace (now known as Disney Springs) ushered in the season with a performance of *The Glory and the Pageantry of Christmas*. It was literally a traditional "living nativity scene" enactment that was originally performed at the open air pavilion known as the Captain's Tower (now Pin Traders) but soon moved to the larger venue of the Waterfront Dock Stage. The shopping area nearby was decorated to suggest a recreation of the little town of Bethlehem.

It was such a popular and dignified show that guests did not mind standing in line for hours for a chance to see it. "The Christmas Story," narrated by Kevin Miles (whose deep baritone voice could also be heard in venues like Epcot's Voices of Liberty and Magic Kindgom's Dapper Dans) and interspersed with Christmas songs, was amazingly simple.

Mary and Joseph approach the manger and she reveals a child wrapped in swaddling clothes. The shepherds appear. The angels appear, rising up from behind the manger. There was a total cast of 36 performers.

The narration told how the shopkeepers of the village brought gifts including cheese from the dairyman and breads from the baker. Sadly, one little orphan child had no gift to bring. To the strains of the song "Little Drummer Boy," a small child walks up to the manger and encouraged by Mary, plays his drum.

There was no official announcement of the reason for the show's cancellation, but there were rumors that it had grown so popular that large audiences caused logistical challenges. There were also grumblings that the show was not substantially increasing sales at the nearby shops.

Acknowledgments

As always, I acknowledge not only the people who directly helped me with this specific book, but those who have inspired or supported me over the years. There are indeed angels in this world and I have been blessed to know so many of them in my life.

I would like to thank all the people who have bought my Disney history books because their continuing support has allowed this book to be published.

This book would not have been possible without the skills and encouragement of publisher Bob McLain and his Theme Park Press.

I acknowledge those sometimes unknown heroes of Disney history who have worked hard to keep the images and facts about extinct Walt Disney World alive for all of us and unfortunately have sometimes had their hard work "borrowed" without proper credit:

- Yesterland is run by Werner Weiss who since 1995 has diligently documented things at both Disneyland and Walt Disney World that went to Yesterland. I can personally attest to Werner's commitment to get the facts right or just not print them.

- Widen Your World. Since around 1996, Mike Lee has been a major source of original information you won't find elsewhere for anyone who loved early WDW.

- Parkeology started by Shane Lindsay in 2009 and then joined by Ted Tamburo always makes me smile with their investigations into the little nooks and crannies of early Walt Disney World.

- Walt Dated World has been operating since 2001 from Mouseketeer Alison with some great photos.

- Lost Epcot. Since 2001, this site has shared accurate information about early Epcot.

In addition, there are other websites and other historians who have written about early Walt Disney World like Jeff Kurtti, Shawn Slater, David Koenig, Sam Gennawey, Cole Geryak, Lou Mongello, Chris Ware, Jack Spence, Kevin Yee, Andrew Kiste, Jim Hill, Christopher Smith and Dave R. Smith among others. They took the time to do the research and were generous in sharing it with the rest of us.

All those listed here have enriched Disney history for all of us and are a constant inspiration to try harder to get the story and get the story right.

Thanks to my brothers, Michael and Chris, and their families, including their children—Amber, Keith, Autumn, and Story. Also, thanks to my grand-nieces Skylar, Shea and Sidnee (Fairbanks) and grand nephews Max (Fairbanks) and Alex (Johansen). None of you read my books but all of you enjoy Walt Disney World.

Thanks to all those who worked at WDW who were so gracious to share with me their memories and point me in the right directions.

About the Author

Jim Korkis is an internationally respected Disney historian who has written hundreds of articles and thirty books about all things Disney over the last forty years. Jim grew up in Glendale, California where starting at the young age of fifteen, he was able to meet and interview some of Walt's original team of animators and Imagineers.

In 1995, he relocated to Orlando, Florida where he worked for Walt Disney World in a variety of capacities including Entertainment, Animation, Disney Institute, Disney University, College and International Programs, Disney Cruise Line, Disney Design Group, Disney Vacation Club, Disney Learning Center, Yellow Shoes Marketing and more.

During that time, he was often tasked with researching and sharing the history of Walt Disney World with cast members and operating participants through presentations and articles. He has written five other books about Walt Disney World.

His original research on Disney history has been used often by the Walt Disney Company as well as other organizations including the Disney Family Museum.

Several websites currently frequently feature Jim's articles about Disney history:

- MousePlanet.com
- AllEars.net
- Yesterland.com
- CartoonResearch.com
- YourFirstVisit.net

In addition, Jim is a frequent guest on multiple podcasts as well as a consultant and keynote speaker to various businesses, schools and groups. He is not an employee of the Disney company.

To read more stories by Jim Korkis about Disney history, please check out his other books, all available from Theme Park Press:

- *The Vault of Walt: Volume 9, Halloween Edition (2020)*
- *Hidden Treasures of the Disney Cruise Line (2020)*
- *Secret Stories of Extinct Disneyland (2019)*
- *The Vault of Walt: Volume 8, Outer Space Edition (2019)*
- *The Unofficial Walt Disney World Companion 1971 (2019)*
- *The Vault of Walt: Volume 7, Christmas Edition (2018)*
- *Secret Stories of Mickey Mouse (2018)*
- *More Secret Stories of Disneyland (2018)*
- *Extra Secret Stories of Walt Disney World (2018)*
- *Call Me Walt (2017)*
- *Walt's Words (2017)*
- *Other Secret Stories of Walt Disney World (2017)*
- *Secret Stories of Disneyland (2017)*
- *The Vault of Walt: Volume 6 (2017)*
- *Gremlin Trouble (2017)*
- *Donald Duck's Daddy (2017)*
- *More Secret Stories of Walt Disney World (2016)*
- *The Vault of Walt: Volume 5 (2016)*
- *The Unofficial Disneyland 1955 Companion (2016)*
- *How to Be a Disney Historian (2016)*
- *Secret Stories of Walt Disney World (2015)*
- *The Vault of Walt: Volume 4 (2015)*
- *Everything I Know I Learned from Disney Animated Features (2015)*
- *The Vault of Walt: Volume 3 (2014)*
- *Animation Anecdotes (2014)*
- *Who's the Leader of the Club? Walt Disney's Leadership Lessons (2014)*
- *The Book of Mouse (2013)*
- *The Vault of Walt: Volume 2 (2013)*
- *Who's Afraid of the Song of the South? (2012)*
- *The Revised Vault of Walt (2012)*

About Theme Park Press

Theme Park Press publishes books primarily about the Disney company, its history, culture, films, animation, and theme parks, as well as theme parks in general.

Our authors include noted historians, animators, Imagineers, and experts in the theme park industry.

We also publish many books by first-time authors, with topics ranging from fiction to theme park guides.

And we're always looking for new talent. If you'd like to write for us, or if you're interested in the many other titles in our catalog, please visit:

www.ThemeParkPress.com

Theme Park Press Newsletter

Subscribe to our free email newsletter and enjoy:

- Free book downloads and giveaways
- Access to excerpts from our many books
- Announcements of forthcoming releases
- Exclusive additional content and chapters
- And more good stuff available nowhere else

To subscribe, visit www.ThemeParkPress.com, or send email to newsletter@themeparkpress.com.

Read more about these books
and our many other titles at:

www.ThemeParkPress.com

United States

Westward Expansion

ISBN: 9798842933679

The Westward Movement of the United States started in the 1500's after the Europeans landed in North America and took land from the Native Americans.